MY NIGHT IN THE MOST HAUNTED HOTEL IN TEXAS

VICTORIA MUNDAE

BEYOND THE FRAY
Publishing

ISBN 13: 978-1-954528-61-1

Cover design: Disgruntled Dystopian Publications

Beyond The Fray Publishing, a division of Beyond The Fray, LLC, San Diego, CA

www.beyondthefraypublishing.com

BEYOND THE FRAY

Publishing

CONTENTS

For all the cats who refused to fit into the boxes they were given

CHAPTER 1

THE VOICES

*T*he room was dark, the air weighing me down beneath my blankets. Heavy. Heavy and damp. The fan hummed continuously, drowning out the sounds from below. Morning light began to gently filter through the weave of the cotton curtains, stretching across my face. I closed my eyes tighter, hoping to block the light, sleep a bit longer. Silently I cursed to myself, wishing I had bought shades with a tighter weave. *It'd block out more light. I could sleep a bit longer,* I thought as I turned over in bed. Try as I might, I could not find more rest.

"Get up. Get your butt up. Get up *now!*"

Hey... I know this voice. I've heard this voice before. I closed my eyes tighter, hoping to shut out the voice. Illogical, I know, but in the early dawn moments, logic does not always rule.

"Get. Up. **NOW!**"

Do you MIND? Geez! This voice doesn't mess around. It's

like a freaking drill sergeant in the army. Insubordinate thoughts began running around inside my brain. I was almost expecting it to scream *"DROP AND GIVE ME 20"* if I did not heed the call, but so far, I've managed to escape the early morning calisthenics. *"Be all you can be"* had nothing on this voice within my brain.

"Ok fine, al-*RIGHT*! I'm *up!*" I said out loud, sitting straight up in bed, hair disheveled and all over my head. I began to look around the room, my eyes starting to focus in the dawn's early light. No one was in the room with me; I waited a moment. "So *why* exactly am I getting up?" I realized I was asking an empty room, but I never want to be rude. I heard a question; I needed to answer.

"We're *go-ing.*"

In true Vulcan fashion, I cocked one eyebrow up. Looking around, trying to casually confirm I was in the room alone, I saw no one. Yep, all alone. Just the cat and I. Although Tobe (named after legendary filmmaker Tobe Hooper) is a superior feline, intelligent as a Rhodes scholar, I do not think he has mastered the art of human speech. At least not yet. However, there were times when he came close. Honestly, I have heard the cat speak to me in small-syllable words. If it was not my small-syllable English-speaking cat, then it had to be the voice in my head. Through my life, this voice has saved me in so many different ways. I have learned to never ignore this voice of wisdom and guidance. Them? I had to stop and think. *Just how many different voices are there inside?*

"Al-righty then," I said aloud to the empty room. "And where are we going, please?"

"We're going to Jefferson. Today."

Hmmm, I thought. *I'm between projects now, and life is, well... I really don't have anything going on these days. If anything is going to shake up these cobwebs in my life, I think it would be a road trip! I mean, I can't think of a reason why I should **not** go. Why not head out on an adventure? Life is what you make it.*

"Okily-dokily, why the *hell* not. Let's go!" And with a declaration of adventure, my feet flailed from beneath the fortress of blankets. I pointed my toes in the direction of the ground and threw my hands up in the air like a five-year-old, sliding out of my oversized bed, and stuck the landing on the carpeted floor.

Over the past few years I have realized there is a difference between hearing and listening. Through the trials of the most recent past, I have trained myself to listen. When the voice says to do something, I get up and do it - *immediately*. If I do not, the voice will get louder. Louder in my head, crescendoing into a scream until I take action. Then it will cease fire. And there I always remained, waiting for the other shoe to fall.

At first I worried that this was not normal, that I was hearing things I should not be hearing. The voices were not quite on the same level as what Joan of Arc heard, but they were my internal instructions. I learned early in my life that ignoring them tended not to be in my best inter-est. As long as I listened and did what they said, I found that I was mysteriously guided along an invisible path, a path that often led me on incredible journeys.

Jefferson? *I know Jefferson!* A small, haunted town in extreme Northeast Texas, but that was all I knew. Quickly, I opened up my laptop and found the listing for the Jefferson Hotel. There I found beautiful pictures of the rooms, some themed, others decorated with antiques, and all containing descriptions beneath the images. I always felt it was somehow cheating in a way, reading up on the venue you are going to be investigating. How could that not subconsciously seep into your psyche, potentially influencing the things you see or witness? Personally, I would much rather go in cold, knowing little of the history, the stories, and the lore of the place. This adventure to Jefferson would not be any different. I chose to instead focus on the photos and my intuition in order to find the room I was most drawn to, and selected that one for my evening's stay.

Being a young girl growing up in the South, I was constantly immersed in a land filled with antiques and history. My eyes had been drawn to one of the last rooms listed - a beautiful room with bright red wallpaper and an antique bed that stretched up, being constrained only by the ceiling. *This* is the room that called out to me. I could feel it; this was the room I was meant to stay in. This was the only room I could have chosen and I eagerly booked it for the night before someone else did. Room 19 was waiting for me!

I have discovered that one of the wonderful things

about having a nontraditional career is that you do not work traditional hours. I found myself on the Wednesday morning before Valentine's Day still single and wanting to get out of town before the realization of yet another romantic holiday spent alone set in. With no one to share the day with, I decided instead to set off for an adventure. After all, Room 19 was waiting for me. I quickly packed a small bag of clothing, grabbed my favorite pieces of ITC equipment, and headed off.

Texas is a wide-open state, crying out to be explored. As a child, I had been told that until everything in Texas had been explored, we could never "vacation" outside of the state. I always thought that was just my dad trying to get out of summer obligations, but in the past few years of my adult life, I have realized how true those words have become. It is because of that *Texas First* mentality, road trips have always been a part of my life. Family road trips were well orchestrated, but as I grew into my teens, I found freedom from the constraints of life by jumping in my car, filling it with gas, grabbing a soda, and heading off on an adventure.

In exploring the state, I began to explore my past, my heritage. Driving down the small, forgotten roads allowed me to open up, to think, to hear the voices clearly. As I slowed and drove through the tired old towns, fragmented memories began to appear, drifting and dancing with the shadows moving across the roads. Little flashes of an echo, an event or an experience, of things I somehow knew, a repressed thought suddenly remembered, facts and events triggered by the farms I passed, buildings that began to look vaguely familiar. I felt I had seen them before, somewhere in my past. I drove forward, one eye on the fuel gauge, one eye on the road, and I began to discover many lost parts of my life. As I began to look and remember, I began to "see".

I left the paved roads of the city for the small back roads of Texas and found myself driving through a landscape that had not changed in decades. The heartbeat of the road, bovines standing along the sides in the fields, unfettered by life beyond the barbed-wire fence and, of course, the obligatory *"mooing"* emanating from my car as I quickly passed the herd. The fundamentals of the road trip. Buildings I recognized from my childhood were soon replaced by unfamiliar sights. The towns grew smaller, with names I had always heard. Important historical names. I found I was no longer going on a road trip; I was living history and traveling back in time. For a while, I drove through memories, unsure if they were mine or residual hauntings from the past, voices left lingering in the light. *Just drive, drive through the filtered sunlight of the pine trees*. Who needs a map when every road takes you home?

What I had not realized was this trip was going to be different. The small black-topped roads would take me through forgotten lands, past houses and buildings crumbling into decay, deeper into the places that were seldom seen by daily drivers. This back-road adventure would take me deeper than I had ever been and would ultimately lead me to a place where I learned to trust the voices I heard and to trust my intuition, eventually helping me to find myself.

~

*A*fter a few hours, the signs along the road indicated the speed limit was growing smaller and smaller. I knew I must be getting close to Jefferson. As I looked out the window to the right, I saw an old railroad trestle bridge spanning the remains of what must have been, at one time, a raging bayou. No longer wild and untamed, the bayou was reduced to a lazy stream of flowing water, flowing along and taking the sands of time downstream. The iron railings of the train trestle were covered with ivy, the tracks no longer there. Nature was taking back the landscape. Shadows were growing longer across the fields and down the banks to the bayou. It was as if they belonged to each other. *This is what peace must look like, as it settles across the land.*

Gently I smiled, driving past the bridge. I began thinking how life must have been at one time. *How simple it must have been here, in this remote part of the state.* The town, nestled in a remote corner of Texas, looks like it has been untouched by modern concerns, an undated snapshot of life in the South. Slowing down to a crawl, I saw a stop sign ahead. This was my chance to turn and to literally go back in time, experiencing what Jefferson was like over 170 years ago.

From 1845 to 1873, Jefferson was one of Texas' most important trade centers, the sixth-largest and second-richest settlement in Texas. The source of the town's wealth was "The Great Raft", a naturally occurring logjam that blocked the upper reaches of the Red River, making a dam that was deep enough to allow for steamboat traffic to pass through the rivers and bayous. Traffic flowed from New Orleans, through Caddo Lake, ending in Big Cypress Bayou, the home of Jefferson's bustling port. Cotton grown on Jefferson's plantations sat in towering bales on the riverside docks. The town hosted an eclectic mixture of plantation aristocrats, European immigrants, merchants, and rivermen. Meat-packing plants, mills and factories sprouted up as far as the eye could see. In the 1860s these factories would help supply the Confederate Army with clothing, iron ore and gunpowder. Even during the federal occupation after the Civil War, in true Texas fashion, Jefferson found a way to not only survive but also thrive. Through this bizarre twist of luck and fate, life in Jefferson exploded.

Thanks to the newly chartered steamboat routes along the bayou, for workers working along the Mississippi, Jefferson quickly became the westernmost part of the water routes that could be reached by boats. It was here in Jefferson goods had to be transferred from the boats maneuvering into Texas and then placed on railroad cars, continuing on their journey across the land.

In what could only be called an ironic twist of fate and history, local settlers tried in vain for years to remove the "Great Red River Raft", but achieved little to no success. Without considering what the future and potential ramifications might be, the Army Corps of Engineers tried one more time to remove the logs that bottled up the waters. In 1873, they used nitroglycerine, a component used in dynamite, to once and for all remove the logjam. It was not until after the logs splintered and the coagulated mud began to fall back down to earth did they see how they changed the fate of the town. The Big Cypress Bayou was drained, the water gone. As the water from the bayou vanished, so did the livelihood of the town. The citizens of Jefferson drained not only the water, they also drained the commerce. Without the waterway trade, the connections to the other bustling towns ceased to exist, and the town of Jefferson began to die. Unable to make a living, the citizens of the town left as well. In what felt like a momentary heartbeat, the population changed and dropped from thirty thousand to near three thousand by the end of the decade.

Everywhere I looked, I was able to imagine what the town must have looked like when it was at its height. It was not until the next day I discovered how significant this bridge crossing over the Big Cypress Bayou was. Built in the 1890s, this bridge had been welded and constructed in Pennsylvania by the Phoenix Bridge Company. It took almost a decade, but slowly the bridge was delivered and reconstructed across the wild Big Cypress Bayou in Jefferson. Forgotten by the hands of time, this is not any bridge;

it is one of the last remaining train trestle bridges in America

So who has remained behind, and who haunts the Jefferson Hotel? Through the years, the hotel has seen more than its fair share of the unexplainable. Guests have reported hearing and seeing two children near the age of seven, a little boy and a little girl. They are believed to be casualties of the building's earlier days when it was a cotton warehouse. Despite their lives being cut short and their untimely deaths, the two children are some of the most high spirited and "lively" (pardon the pun) inhabitants at the hotel. Often they can be heard laughing and chasing each other through the halls as children should, living life forever as a child, untethered, young and free.

For as long as I can remember, there have been spirits of little children around me. I have always been able to connect with children. Many times they have shown up in photos next to me, always about hip level. I often wondered if it was because I was a mother? Could they tell? Or was it because of my Girl Scout leader tenure? Did I give off that aura? Whatever the reason, children seem to trust me; they find me, staying close at hand and knowing they will be safe if I am near. At times I felt like a paranormal babysitter, but then I stop and remember, they *chose* to visit with me, and for that, I am grateful. I could not help but wonder, would I be able to make contact with the children of the Jefferson?

CHAPTER 2

JEFFERSON

*O*nly two blocks away, I caught sight of the outline of the Jefferson Hotel. Standing silently like a forgotten memory from the past, the large hotel looked out of place. As I drove closer, the building became more in focus, and I began feeling the eyes. Eyes that were peering through the lace sheers that covered every window on the street. I could sense there were souls behind them, keenly watching as I moved closer to the hotel. The Jefferson Hotel was draped in a crown of wrought iron, making it stand out, separate from the other buildings that lined the street, resembling a building that should have been found in New Orleans somewhere near the French Quarter. The hotel was a juxtaposition in time, mysteriously finding its home deep in Texas.

At last, I finally reached my destination. Turning the car off, I sat for a moment, taking in the sights of the town. I stepped out of my car and began to gather my bags. Then I noticed it. I noticed the quiet of the street. It was three o'clock in the middle of the week, yet no one could be seen on the streets or in the buildings. Nowhere. Suddenly I realized I had not seen anyone since I turned off the main road and headed down a smaller street and into town. When things such as this happen, I have always wondered and began to ask myself... Did something happen? Was the town evacuated, and I just did not know it? Is there a reason why there are no people walking around? This must be what a *true* ghost town looks like. It sure feels like one.

A new person in a small town always tends to stand out. As I got out of my car, one of the doors of the hotel popped open, the first signs of human life I had seen in about twenty minutes. A very energetic man emerged, and I was greeted by the owner of The Historic Jefferson Hotel. "Hi there! You checking in?" he asked as he began to walk across the street, not bothering to look in either direction for oncoming traffic. *I suppose they don't do traffic here.*

"Yes, but I'm a few minutes early, though. Is that okay?" I replied. It was twenty minutes until check-in, but considering I drove halfway across Texas, I would consider that being on time.

"Oh, yeah, sure. C'mon in!" he said. I walked across the street and introduced myself. He punched in a code to the door. I was reassured knowing that not anyone could "just walk in". Only those who were invited could enter; I felt safe from curious onlookers and vampires who might be in the vicinity.

He was high-energy and full of life, introducing himself and his wife, and was excited that I was staying the night with them. The owner gave me a moment to look around as I walked up to the front desk. There were so many things to see, so many lights and colors in the room. *I must look like a kid in a paranormal candy store.* Wide-eyed and sensory overloaded, I stopped to take it all in. Never have I been one to pull a phone out and start taking photos. In fact, most of the time I overpack my ITC equipment and then forget to use it. I am absorbed in the moment, taking it all in, feeling the energy of the room.

Usually the voices are excited as well, so there is always a constant narrative running through my head. In a situation such as this, when the energy, vibrations, lights, and colors are so active, all the voices begin clamoring in my brain, talking over each other, and I have to stop and try to hear what they are all saying. When that has happened previously to me, I normally reach for something to touch, a chair, a wall, a doorframe, an attempt to ground myself so I will not fly off. Or at least that is the way it feels. Connect to this reality and this place in time, and then allow the voices, the messages, and the sights to fly around and through me. I would much rather *have* a paranormal experience than to try to *document* one.

I signed in on the register. I cannot remember the last time I signed in to a place where I was staying. *Nice touch.*

Old-world charm, I like that. The owner walked around the desk, and we each grabbed a bag and began to walk towards the wooden staircase. I stopped, looking around and soaking it all in. The owner took the lead and showed me upstairs, narrating our journey and revealing the names of the different rooms as we passed by the open doors. Exchanging pleasantries as we ascended the steep, creaking staircase, he asked if I knew the history of the hotel. I confessed to him that I knew nothing about it. I did not exactly want to tell the owner of the hotel that the little voice inside my head had told me to get up and drive to Jefferson, but I sheepishly admitted that I knew the hotel was haunted but that was the extent of it.

He seemed rather surprised that I had not explored the stories before driving up for my stay. I told him someone I knew had stayed here once a year or so ago, and she said it was fantastic. *"So much activity,"* she said, but she had a tendency to overexaggerate and say that about everything, but I kept those details to myself. *"It was a great hotel,"* and I definitely had to, *"check it out sometime."* But that was all I knew about the hotel and Jefferson.

The first thing I noticed when I reached the top of the stairs was how long the hall was. Sunlight streamed through the stained glass of the door at the end of the hallway. The afternoon sun gave everything a beautiful glow of burnt sienna and a blinding shine. I was sure this is what a memory of the past, of the Wild West, must look like. Sepia in nature, the hall was timeless. By looking at the walls, the floor, one could not tell what year they were in. If it were not for the security camera and electric lighting, I could have sworn that I had been transported back into the earliest days of the hotel.

Everywhere you turned, there were antiques, a most eclectic collection of a lifetime. *The Smithsonian doesn't hold a candle to this. I wonder if there is an audio tour that goes along with this. Nah, probably not.* It would have taken an entire night just to walk through and look at everything, and even then, I am sure I would have missed a lot. The devil is in the details, I've always heard.

The long, thin wooden floorboards began to creak as we walked down the hallway. They were the original floorboards from a building that was over 170 years old. It has been painstakingly restored and ornately decorated, and the love of the restoration shone through. Each unoccupied room had the door open. A red velvet rope stretched across each door, barring entry to any room. As with any haunted venue, there was of course a room filled with dolls. Along my way down the hall I saw a circus room, a railroad room, an elaborate room of mirrors, and a nautical room. Room 19 was at the end of the hall on the left and adjacent to a large Egyptian sarcophagus. While walking to my room, I passed the Fiji Mermaid, clown heads, a random photograph of Dave Schrader, large rabbits, and blinking lights. The Jefferson was beginning to take on a carnival atmosphere.

As we made our way down the hall, I learned a bit about the history of the building, but nothing about the hauntings. The owner was very careful not to tell me what others have seen and experienced, knowing I wanted to "find out on my own". I was curious and wanted to see what I could encounter and pick up just from my own cognitive abilities. For many reasons, I am very thankful that he did not disclose his more famous eternal residents. I wonder if I would have made it through the night had the owner divulged all the secrets of the Jefferson.

Diagonal from the room I was staying in was another room named the "Pride Room". The Pride Room was an homage to the Pride House, the first bed and breakfast in Texas, filled with stained-glass windows that were original to the Pride, a wooden bed, and memorabilia from the bed and breakfast. We stopped for a moment to look inside. The owner told me the Pride Bed and Breakfast was a large gabled Victorian mansion built in 1888. In 1901, there was a fire that destroyed a large part of the building and also claimed the life of the owner's young daughter. In true Texas pioneer spirit, the Pride had been rebuilt and opened again. I stood for a moment at the entrance of the room, my eyes caught in the refracted light of the stained glass that hung inside, dangling down from the ceiling. There was a feeling of comfort on the other side of the red velvet rope, and for a moment, I relaxed.

Finally, we turned to the room I was staying in. *At last!* Room 19 was the last room at the end of the very long hall. All the way at the end of the hotel. Far, far away. The owner walked forward, removing the red velvet rope that guarded my room from any living human entry.

"So you know about this room, right?" he asked. I shook my head no. He looked at me and asked why I chose the room. Smiling and thinking of all the rooms I had to choose from, why **did** I select this room? I really did not want to say *"oh, those voices. They told me to pick this room"*. People will begin to look at you in a particular way when you mention the voices in your head speaking to you, offering their cerebral advice and wisdom. Instead I told him it was the room with the prettiest bed, and I really wanted to stay in there. *Man, that's so lame. Couldn't you think of anything better to say? You sound like an airhead. Why not blink your eyes and seal that package?*

With the seriousness of a mortician, he told me it was called the "Bride's Room". *Great*, I thought. *That's the place I want to stay, especially right before Valentine's Day. In the Bride's Room. I guess the framed wedding dress on the wall should have been the first clue.*

He went on to tell me about the "Jilted Bride", how she received a message on her wedding day saying her fiancé was not coming and that he had never had any intention of showing up. Distraught and overwhelmed, she found a rope, tied it to the top of the headboard, and took her own life. The current owners have moved the bed into three different rooms, and guests keep reporting the same activity no matter which room the bed is in.

"Oh, how *awful*. Uh… this is a new mattress, *right?*" I joked, trying to lighten the mood. He did not smile. *Wow, tough crowd. Note to self, he's serious about the paranormal. Duly noted.*

"Let's see," the owner said quite stoically. "This is Wednesday, right? We had a man staying here Monday night, in this room. He didn't make it through the night. Just left the key on the front desk," he said.

I could feel my eyes opening wide with curiosity. I could feel my head tilting like a puppy that just does not understand. "What happened? Did he see something? Did something happen?" I asked.

"I don't know," he said matter-of-factly. "He just up and ran out during the middle of the night. I have no idea what happened. Anyway... you're the only one who checked in for tonight... so have a look around! Just be careful and enjoy yourself!" he said. "We're going to run a few errands, but we'll be back in a little bit. Here's my number. If you need anything, just text me."

You're leaving me here? Alone? By myself? ALL BY MYSELF? Well, at least the door has a lock and a code. And it is still daylight. I guess I'll be okay.

I smiled. I had a feeling my smile looked like a mashup of the *Mona Lisa* and the Cheshire cat. He handed me the key to my room, turned, and walked down the hall, the creaking boards trailing behind him and growing fainter and more distant as he disappeared down the staircase.

Inside Room 19 The Haunted Bride's Room

CHAPTER 3

THE WALKABOUT

*A*fter settling into my room, I decided to go on a walkabout. What a perfect opportunity, the only (living) guest in the building. I felt I could explore with ease.

Looking around the room, the first thing I noticed was the very large headboard on the bed. I began to wonder how someone could hang themselves from the top of it. The headboard is very tall, peaking at the center and almost touching the ceiling. It could have easily been ten feet tall.

"Hello," I said out loud to an empty room. "My name is Victoria, and thank you for allowing me to stay in your room. I'm very sorry for what happened, but I can totally understand." I continued speaking with her, to anyone who was in the room, trying to reassure them that I was just here to visit. It was my hope that we could connect. I imagined her grief and despair coupled with the constant unrequited love I seem to encounter would instantly make us besties. "I'll be here all night," I said. "We can chat later if you want."

In my mind's eye I began hearing and seeing a little girl speaking in a singsong voice. Over and over she sang, *"My name is Jen-nny... my name is Jen-nny"*. From what I could see, Jenny appeared to be somewhere in her "tween" years, light-colored hair, which was twisted and curled and pulled back at the crown of her head. She was wearing a white cotton dress that fell just below the knees. The dress had a dropped waist and squared collar, which was decorated with elaborate stitching. She was not wearing any shoes, but honestly, neither was I. *Texas girls, always barefoot.* Her attire could have easily been from the early 1900s. Jenny was quite clear in my third eye, and she was loud in my ear. *Does the third eye have an ear? Do we have a third ear? How do you describe to others that you hear voices and sounds with your inner eye and not with your inner ear? Have I learned to circumvent the cochlea?* I sat on the edge of the bed, facing the small closet, and listened to Jenny singing her name.

Jenny had her hands on the front of her dress and lifting it slightly, she began swaying back and forth while continuing to sing her name. Something any child would do who is playing. Not wanting to be rude, I said hello to her and I returned to unpacking my bag. I have made it a practice to always say hello, no matter if it is a ghost, spirit, person, plant or animal. I feel there are three things any living (or "living") entity ever really craves - to be heard, to be validated and to be loved. Using these three principles, I formed my own group, *WyldWood Paranormal - giving voices to those who cannot speak.* Living or departed, we are all the same. We want to be heard and validated.

Reaching for my digital recorder, I decided I was going to go for a walk. I slipped the recorder in the pocket of my jeans. I have managed to capture many EVPs over the years, usually while I am just talking out loud to whomever might be in the room. I have learned to trust my intuition, to trust what I see in my mind's eye. Ghosts are people too, for the most part, and I do not feel the paranormal exists for our entertainment. I also do not feel that we need to "prove" the existence of the paranormal. *Please stop asking them to perform on command. There is no need to ask the paranormal to light up lights on a K2 meter, ask the same repetitive questions time and time again.*

The paranormal is another dimension that exists, just as air and gravity exist in our current daily life. The after-life is a normal part of life. Perhaps it is the part of life that we are not always aware of or have not developed an ability to see daily. I do feel strongly that we have reached a time when we no longer need to "prove". Instead I feel we should be experiencing and understanding.

I gathered the key to the room and walked to the door, which was still open to the hallway. *I guess I really don't need to lock the door,* I thought. *Hell, I probably don't even need to close the door. I mean, after all, I'm the only one here. And if a ghost wants to get in, will the door really stop them?*

I have learned from the activity that I have in my own

personal home, always take the key with you. So many times the car door will lock on my car after sitting for hours alone in the garage, and always just as I start to get near the car door. Back inside I go, fetching the car keys from the keyholder on the wall. This is one way the spirits in my home have their giggles, letting me know they are still here. With that thought, I journeyed into the hall and began to look around.

Across the hall from the Bride's Room was a room called the "Bootlegger's Room". Just as you step into the Bootlegger's Room, there is an area of the floor that opens up and exposes a hidden staircase that goes down. In the 1920s and 1930s, prohibition existed in Texas. Speakeasies and gin joints were hidden in plain sight all over the country, and Texas was no different. They were common and easy to find. You just needed to know how to look for them.

Removing the red velvet rope from the door, I entered and carefully looked around the room, making sure not to fall into the oubliette in the floor. The room was sparsely decorated and appeared to be still under construction, and repairs were continuing. *When it's finished, it's going to be magnificent!* I thought. Careful not to disturb anything, I looked around the room and then left. This room is at the end of the hall, directly across from the room I was staying in, Room 19. There was a stained-glass door at the very end of the hall, and I stopped to look out the window.

While looking out the window, I became aware of a

man standing at the other end of the hall, near the staircase that led up to the attic and up to the Spirit Room (or
the Room of Despair as it was named here). I could tell the
man was standing at the foot of the second staircase, one
foot on the bottom step and holding on to the rail. He was
leaning around the banister, looking at me. I had a feeling
that he was trying to figure out who was at the end of the
hall, if it was someone he knew. I was aware I was alone in
the building, so this had to be a ghost or some form of a
spirit. Concentrating with my third eye, I began looking
at him without turning around, trying to remember his
details.

He was rather tall, an older gentleman, with a very
long, angular face. He had deep-set wrinkles, silvery dark
hair, which was thin and slicked back, eyes that were open
wide and deep set, deep lines across his forehead. He was
wearing dark trousers and a long dark jacket. One that
stopped at the back of his knees. He was also wearing a
vest, which was buttoned, and a string tie that hung
loosely in front of his white shirt. He had a hat on. Not
exactly a top hat, not exactly a cowboy hat. But it was
something with a brim, not too tall and dark. I thought he
must have been going up the second staircase, getting
ready for the evening or a night of haunting, when he
noticed me at the other end of the hall. I could see that his
arm was bent, and he had something draped over it. To
me it looked like a heavier coat. *I mean, why not? After all, it
was going to be very cold tonight.*

I did not feel he was evil at all; he reminded me of

something. But what? Then I realized he was a perfect combination between Matt Dillon from *Gunsmoke* and "The Gentleman" from *Buffy the Vampire Slayer.*

I think I will wait a bit before going down the hall. I'm perfectly fine standing down here at the other end, just looking out the window. Hey, look at that building over there; oh, was that a bird? I continued thinking to myself, pretending to be interested in everything outside. *As long as he stays down there, I think I'm okay. I'll just wait here and pretend I'm looking out the window and enjoying the scenery.*

After a few moments, I no longer felt him at the end of the hall, watching me. I thought it was safe to turn around and continue on my journey.

*How cool is **this**? I've only been here a few minutes and I've already had two encounters with ghosts. And in the middle of the afternoon at that!*

Carefully I continued down the hallway, walking in bare feet. The boards were creaking, sounding as if they would break at any moment. *This must be what an old pirate ship sounded like, minus the crashing waves, of course.* I thought walking in bare feet would help me navigate down the hall. I could feel the board if it were to give way, and I would know if I needed to move quickly before I fell through a broken board, ending up in the room below. I have already had that experience somewhere else. Not a fun thing to do, so I thought I would do everything possible to keep history from repeating, but just at a different place. Thankfully all the boards held. I would pause momentarily at each room, stretching as far as I could over the red velvet rope. Some things I couldn't see clearly, so I gingerly took down the rope, stepping in a few feet just to have a look around.

This is the most uniquely decorated haunted hotel. A lifetime of collecting the most interesting and unique artifacts. Circus oddities, pop culture, and the paranormal meld into the motif.

CHAPTER 4

❧

THE DOLL ROOM

*D*olls. *Why are there always dolls?* As a young child, I had dolls to play with and to keep me entertained. Such elaborate plots my dolls would conjure up. For days I would play out a narrative that could almost rival the works of Shakespeare.

Annabelle, Chucky, Talking Tina, and clowns. We have a fear of dolls. Pediophobia is the clinical term for our irrational fear. Frightened of puppets? That's pupaphobia.

As one would expect, the Jefferson Hotel has a room dedicated to dolls. It is the first thing you notice when you reach the top of the stairs. It is an amazing collection of vintage dolls in all shapes and sizes, in various poses. I imagined they froze as they were when they heard us coming up the staircase, but that is just ridiculous. Isn't it? The room is brightly decorated in beautiful colors, giving the dolls a wonderful place to live. But for whatever reason, even though I played with dolls as a child, dolls today creep me out.

Not wanting to be rude, I stopped at the door and looked inside. *Yeah, this is one room I don't really want to go inside. How can people possibly sleep in here? I mean, there are dolls hanging from the ceiling... upside down.* I soon discovered that many of the themed rooms had items suspended from the ceilings. I can understand how that would psychologically throw a guest off balance. I tip my hat to the owners, metaphorically, for adding a fun house element and creating the perfect environment for a very haunted hotel.

Sticking my head inside the door, barely beyond the red velvet rope, I said hello to everyone, telling the dolls it was nice to meet them. It pays to always be polite, especially in a haunted environment. For some reason, the dolls did not respond. A few of the residents of the room seemed vaguely familiar to me, reminding me of the dolls my sister played with when we were children. She always loved the larger "baby dolls", as we called them. I was always more intrigued with the smaller, handheld Barbie version. Barbies were not as terrifying to me as the "baby doll" genre. I did not hear any dolls screaming at me, as dolls quite often do. No one told me to "get out" or "leave", so I politely asked if I could snap a few photos. I **always** ask before taking a photo. That's Paranormal Etiquette 101. Even before I enter a house for an investigation, I either knock or ask if I may come inside. Maybe I am odd in that way. Maybe it is just a throwback to old Southern manners. Perhaps that is why I never feel frightened when I am involved with an investigation. Again, it is just another part of validation. I acknowledge the spirits and the lives that have lived here, who may have a connection to the dolls in residence. They seemed agreeable enough, so I snapped a few photos.

After spending a few moments with the dolls, I decided to take my leave and turned to continue down the hallway. Directly in front of me was the staircase where I saw the man earlier. I did not see him there this time. It did not feel different; there was no energy shift or heaviness. Yes! I was certain he was no longer there. I did feel a heaviness above me and I knew he was upstairs, in the attic. *That's fine by me. I won't be going up THERE!*

I continued walking slowly down the hallway, trying to take all the sights in as well. I had only moved between eight to ten feet from the Doll Room, not yet reaching the door to the next room. The hotel was silent. There was not a sound coming from the streets. No traffic or sounds of life could be heard anywhere. It was unusually interesting, hearing the loudness of silence. Just as I lifted a foot to take a step, I heard something behind me, stopping me dead in my tracks.

One of the dolls in the Doll Room had begun to giggle softly, repeatedly. *Oh, it must be motion activated,* I thought, trying to placate myself. In situations such as this, I have found comfort in looking for a rational and logical answer to explain or "debunk" an experience before I run willy-nilly, jumping straight into the "it's a ghost!" frame of mind. Weird that it waited until after I left the area before it started giggling. *Hmmm, it must be on some type of motion sensor with a response delay. Well played, Jefferson Hotel. Well played.*

CHAPTER 5

⌘

THE ARMOIRE OF DEATH

*C*ontinuing down the hall, I stopped to admire the eclectic items that surrounded me. A jeweled replica of a Faberge egg, a sculpture that reminded me of *The Sorcerer's Apprentice*, flying dragons suspended from above, green-eyed cats, and rabbit heads hanging on the walls. *Rabbit heads? Again with the rabbit heads?! Why are there so many rabbit heads?* In another room, a train suspended from the ceiling ran upside down. A definite religious theme ran through the upstairs hallway, stained-glass windows, crucifixes, a tapestry of *The Last Supper* where one disciple had a rather pointed ear and an uplifted brow, reminiscent of Mr. Spock from *Star Trek*.

I meandered silently down the hall; it was like gliding through history. I found myself downstairs, being quiet so I would not disturb the dead that still called the hotel home. Carefully looking into each room, I was amazed at the intricacies of the items that lay inside each chamber.

Walking past the Crystal Palace Ballroom, I began seeing, with my third eye, women in beaded dresses spinning and dancing in the brightly lit room. There was an air of happiness and festivity inside the ballroom. I turned and began to walk farther down the hall. The downstairs rooms seemed like a more traditional historic hotel; large mahogany beds accompanied hardwood floors that were original to the building. I stopped to look in one room in particular, where the canopy bed stretched to the ceiling. It was a perfect example of a time that has now gone by. I remember seeing beds such as this in other historic homes I visited when I was a child. *What it must have been like living in a world such as this,* I thought, smiling to myself.

Standing near the red velvet rope that stretched across the door, I found myself smiling again. I wondered what it was like to live in such a magnificent place. Caught up in the moment, I decided to "experience" and not try to "document" everything. You lose so much by staring through the lens of a camera and not watching the life unfolding before your eyes. I walked a few feet farther and stopped in the middle of the hall. I had a feeling there was someone behind me, but knew I was still alone. The voices warned me; something was happening. Ever so casually, I turned around and looked behind. The red velvet rope no longer extended stationary across the door. Instead, the rope was swinging back and forth, in and out of the room, as if invisible hands were turning a jump rope. *Okay-y-y-y,* I thought to myself. There has to be some sort of air movement.

I began looking around for a fan or ductwork in the ceiling that would create a small breeze, giving cause for the movement of the rope. Back and forth, back and forth, swinging back and forth. I looked everywhere, but there was nothing. There was absolutely no logical reason why it should be moving in and out of the door frame. When I could find no logical reason as to why the rope should be rocking, I chuckled to myself and said hello to whomever was making the rope sway. It always pays to be polite. There was definite activity in this hotel, and it seemed with each event the activity was stepping up a small degree.

Thinking to myself, and to the voices inside my head, I began to wonder. *Am I being tested? Why do I feel like I'm being tested? Are the spirits here testing me, trying to see at what point I run out of the building? I can't run out of the building! It's cold outside! Maybe it's the BUILDING doing the haunting? How else can you explain the activity getting stronger each time? I mean, it's not like the ghosts have a checklist to follow. Why would paranormal activity start out gentle and then amp up each time?*

This was the moment when I could really use a cat. I needed the feline paranormal validation. Whenever I would hear or see something in my own home and one of the cats would look over to the same place, I always felt a bit better. Animals are sensitive and have an innate ability, picking up on things we cannot see or hear. There was always a sense of safety and substantiation when one of the cats would respond to my perceived paranormal events. Somehow, I had the feeling that if one of the cats were here, they would be hiding under a bed by now.

Continuing on, I journeyed a little bit farther down the hall. I found a beautiful armoire recessed in the side of the wall. I carefully opened the armoire to peek inside, and to my amazement, I found a set of stairs! *Well, I just gotta*, I said to myself, and much like *Alice Through the Looking Glass* or Lucy walking through the magical wardrobe, I was confident I was going to be transported on a magical journey. Stepping inside, I closed the door behind me and looked into the blue light ahead.

Instead of being transported to Narnia, my claustrophobia was actualized. The magical staircase morphed into a ladder with a ninety-degree twist. *Well, I can't back out now; I'm Facebook live!* Suddenly ten eyeballs popped up on my phone, so I knew at least ten viewers would know if I were to get stuck or die. I felt like Geraldo, but this definitely was not *The Mystery of Al Capone's Vaults*. I flashed back to growing up near NASA, growing up in Space City, and climbing up a rusted rocket slide as a child (and also later in life as a college senior, but that is another story for another time). *The things we did as kids! We ran up the ladders, usually barefoot. Those rocket slides of my youth were three stories tall, but did our parents care? No, it does not appear so. We are all still alive to tell the tales.*

I continued up the hidden wooden ladder. *I hope in time someone finds my corpse. Just look for me sealed in an armoire, going nowhere but up.*

With no other option than to continue on, thanks in

part to the peer pressure of the ten eyeballs of Facebook Live, I managed to make my way up the unevenly spaced rungs on the ladder. I felt a cold breeze gently blow past my face. *Gr-r-reat*, I thought to myself. *If that's a ghost, well, we're both screwed. There's not enough room in here for the both of us. I flashed back to the Presidential Fitness Tests I had been forced to take in elementary school. Gawd, how I hated those.*

Hanging on for dear life, and also for the ten eyeballs, I tilted my head up and saw an opening in the ceiling above. *Oh, sweet Jeezus! There's an escape from this level of Dante's Hell!* I continued ascending the ladder. After two rungs up, I realized I was being birthed into one of the themed rooms! I can only imagine this must have looked like a poor re-enactment of the great escape scene from Stephen King's novella *The Shawshank Redemption*. I emerged through the hole of the floor and into the room. *"Wha the Hell-l-l-l?"* I asked aloud. Or maybe I was asking the voices in my head? Turning to look back into the trapdoor that was open in the floor, I realized I had climbed through the bootlegger's secret passage! Standing inside the Bootlegger's Room on terra firma, I looked directly through the door. Across the hall, I saw my luggage sitting beside the bed with the high headboard. Room 19 was directly in view.

CHAPTER 6

PARANORMAL FROGGER

*I*n what could only be equated to a game of Paranormal Frogger, I dashed across the hall, sliding into Room 19. *Ha! Tom Cruise has nothing on me. Home at last!* I closed the red oriental door behind me (no need to lock it, I am still alone) and walked over to the bed.

Having survived the harrowing situation of the Bootlegger's Armoire o' Death, I decided it was time for me to take a break, relax a bit. I decided I would prowl around later in the evening, and stretched across the bed, pulling my laptop over to me. I could not help but look up at the top of the headboard. A sudden sadness came over me, and I realized... someone killed themselves directly above my head. I was not sure if I was feeling waves of her grief or my own, but I sat silently for a moment, a small tear in the corner of my eye. *I'm so sorry you felt like you weren't loved. You know you were. And I'm so sorry. You deserved so much more out of life.* I continued on, talking to her, identifying with her and with her pain. I am not sure what I said to her after that, but I did speak with her for a few minutes, and before I realized it, I had tears streaming down my cheeks. I knew those were not my tears, but they were hers. Slowly, I was making contact with her, and the voices shifted in my head. I could hear her clearly. I began to understand why she still grieves and how she is forever haunted by her last decision.

~

For me, I see images inside my head. It has always been that way. I remember being three years old and telling my mom that I had a "movie screen inside my head". I would see "movies" and I just did not understand them. As per the norm, she would dismiss me, telling me to be quiet, it was just my imagination. It was not until I was in college did I finally understand what I was seeing. I thought what I was viewing was a form of "double vision", but in reality it was my third eye. Sometimes the images are strong (consequently making driving rather hard at times); some images are faded but can still be seen. Over the years I have been able to push the visions over to one side of my frontal lobe, accessing the information by tilting my head down and looking up "inside" my brain. That is where the voices reside too. I imagine it is like a little paranormal tropical getaway in my head. It is here where I saw what was keeping her so unhappy.

The stories are a bit confusing, and there is not a general consensus as to who the "Jilted Bride" actually was. Oddly enough, there are stories of two different women, fifty years apart. On what should have been the happiest day of their lives, both brides received messages from their betrothed. Messages that said the men were not coming. Not to the hotel. Not to the wedding. Both brides, feeling devastated and beside themselves, took their own lives by hanging from the top of this beautiful bed, which is now in Room 19. The story continues, saying that both brides were reported to be expecting. Did two women have the same lot in life, or have the stories been confused?

Incidents of tapping on the headboard have been reported, while other guests have seen an apparition of a woman in a wedding dress standing at the foot of the bed. Forever known as "the Jilted Bride", their energies are literally tied to the bed, haunting it for eternity. Couple their energy with the former courtesan whose murder was actually documented in this room, and Room 19 has become an energy hot spot for those who reside in the land of unrequited love.

The message I received was from a bride, but which bride I could not tell you. The message was loud and clear. She was in pain. The pain of that final decision still haunts her, pardon the pun. She can never find relief from this pain because she is constantly referred to as "the Jilted Bride". Loud and clear I could hear her. *"I don't like being called the 'Jilted Bride'. It hurts. I know that is my lot in life, to be called that, but it hurts."*

All the sadness returns, the desperation and the hurt feelings resurface. As one might expect, she is not fond of male travelers, especially ones who are traveling alone. I suspect that might have been the case earlier in the week when a man, traveling alone, stayed in Room 19 and left in the middle of the night without explanation. That was the first thought that popped into my head when the owner told me that the previous guest had left quickly.

I spoke aloud to her for a while, asking what I could do to help. Over and over I heard the sobbing message *"I just wanted to be loved. I just wanted to be loved".* It occurred to me that perhaps a nice gesture might ease her pain, but I doubt if it will ever be erased. I told her I had an idea, and I would ask the owner later when I saw him, hoping it would help her out.

I did not hear any more from her, so I returned to stretching across the bed. I had spent several hours driving across Texas earlier in the day and I had a lot of catching up to do. Propping myself up against the headboard, I began to answer the messages and emails of the day. After returning a few messages, I noticed the sun had dropped below the horizon and darkness was all around. It was getting close to dinnertime, so I searched online to see what was near. I was sure the owners must be back from their errands by now.

It was incredibly quiet up on the second floor, all by myself. The only sound I heard was the passing train every forty minutes. Enjoying the quiet, I leaned my head back against the headboard of the bed.

After a few moments, I realized the bed was shaking. *Is the train going by?* I opened one eye and looked around the room, apparently so I could hear better.

No, there's no train. I don't hear a big truck going down the street either. I don't hear the compressor coming on. I had heard it earlier, but not this time. *I am not even sure where it is located, but I seriously doubt if it would make a room shake every time it turned on. We don't have earthquakes. There's no inclement weather happening, other than the cold.* I tried to logically rationalize every scenario that could make the bed shake and came up empty-handed.

Maybe I'll just shoot a text downstairs, see if this is a normal thing.

"Hey there. Victoria here," I began, sending a text to the owner. "So, I'm sitting on the bed, and it feels like someone is pressing up and down with their hands on the mattress, kinda jiggling the mattress. Is that a thing? That's a thing, right? Is that normal?"

I waited a few moments, and then I saw the dancing dots. I knew a reply was on its way. "No. Not usually," came the reply.

Hmmmm, I thought. "*Ok, thanks.*" I did not want them to worry about me, especially since I was alone. When I checked in, they did seem a bit surprised that I was here by myself, not knowing the history and hauntings of the hotel. Couple that with no one else checking in... I think they were watching out for me and made sure I was alright. I was really touched by that. *The kindness of strangers.*

I continued searching on my computer for dinner places and also playing around on the laptop for a bit. About four feet from where I was resting was a built-in dresser which had a flat-screen television and a lamp sitting on it. There were a few glass knickknacks on the dresser, so I made sure to put nothing on it when I came into the room. I did not want to disturb anything; I try to be polite when I am visiting. As a general rule in life, I do not watch television, so the remote was still sitting beside the television on top of the dresser. I giggled at the bed-shaking incident. *How long had it been shaking before I noticed it? If an invisible presence was trying to scare me, they really needed to do a little bit better.* I was impressed though. It was definitely a step up from the giggling doll and the velvet rope that swung by itself.

Then it happened! Something that made me take note! From behind the television came a very audible sound. Three loud, rhythmic strikes on the table. Very loud, very distinct, very clear. *Rap... Rap... Rap!* My eyes opened wide, and I turned my head slowly towards the sound. While the knocking startled me, I did not jump. There was only an inch or so from the back of the television to the wall. Not even room for a fist to fit, much less room for a fist to knock.

"Well, helloooooooo there!" I said aloud in my best imitation Seinfeld voice. I turned and looked in the direction of the knocking. "It's nice to meet you," I said, smiling at the dresser. I stopped typing and waited, directing my full attention to the dresser. It was the polite thing to do, giving them my full attention, hoping the knocking would happen again. I did not ask for them to repeat the knock. *If that's really you, can you knock again? How insulting that must be to those who are in the spirit world. Why, of course it's me. Who were you expecting?*

No further knocks came from the table so I returned to my laptop, internally screaming inside my head. **OHMERGAWD! THIS IS SO FREAKING EXCITING!** I played poker for years and have been told I have a great poker face because I smile all the time. Friends have said that it is hard to get a read on me, but trust me, the gears inside are spinning like crazy. I think I will send another text downstairs.

"*Hi there! Victoria here!*" I started again. "*So... There were just three loud knocks on the dresser, behind the TV. That's a normal thing, right?*"

Again I waited for the dancing dots. Soon they appeared, followed by the answer from the owner.

"No. Not usually. We've all been downstairs. You're the only one up there." I could feel the *Mona Lisa*/Cheshire cat mashup spreading across my face again.

"*Ok, thanks,*" I replied. I asked if he could show me,

after I got back from dinner, the videos we had discussed earlier in the day. The owner was very kind and said he would be happy to show them to me. He has a collection of fun pieces of evidence that the hall cameras have captured. Sounded like a great way to top off the evening.

CHAPTER 7

DARKNESS FALLS

The sun set quickly, faster than I had imagined it would. By the time I had reassembled myself, the town was already blanketed in darkness. *I guess I'll just set out on my own, even if it is all dark... and deserted. Just how many people live here anyway?* I was not afraid of the things that could go bump in the night, but I was not comfortable walking around all alone in a town I did not know after sunset. I wanted to take in the sights, but the sights had disappeared into the darkness.

The night was black, no stars, no moon. I could feel the moisture hanging in the air, so I knew there had to be a river somewhere nearby. I remembered passing over the little bayou and began to wonder if there was a larger part of the river. One that I did not see on the drive into town? *Where the hell is the water... I know there's water... somewhere*, I muttered to myself. Perhaps this stems from a past life experience or two that I partially remember, but I have always had an irrational fear of driving off the road in the middle of the night and crashing into waters I could not see. This night, my senses were tingling, and I knew to beware of the road before me, aware of my surroundings, suspicious of every dark patch.

I decided to hop into my little car and take a drive around the area. I felt safer, and the temperature was beginning to fall quickly. Even though my dining destination was only four blocks away, I felt safer and much warmer driving the distance. This town was incredibly dark; the streetlights did nothing other than cast shadows on top of shadows. Knowing there was water nearby that I could not see, I drove slowly, often not even stepping on the gas, and stopped in the middle of the road at times to look at the historic buildings that silently lined the streets. There were no cars around. It seemed as if I were the only person in the town. At least the only person moving.

I found a nice little bar-slash-restaurant and decided that would be the choice for the night. Walking up the steps, I could feel the history radiating from the walls of the building. I was confident it had seen great things in its lifetime. Opening the door, the first thing I noticed was the ambiance enveloping the cordial and friendly people inside. I sat at the bar and chatted with the bartenders, having a nice warm dinner while we talked about the town.

Of course, not knowing my face, they asked politely what I was doing in Jefferson. *Oh, you know what it's like, the voices in your head... you just do what they tell you to do.*

Mine told me to get up and come to Jefferson. No, I can't tell them that. Vacation? On a Wednesday? Nah, no one would believe that either, I argued with myself.

"Oh, I just took a drive. I've heard so many nice things about Jefferson, I thought I'd just come and check it out." Phew, they seemed ok with that explanation.

Instantly becoming ambassadors of the town, the two ladies behind the bar began pitching the wonders and the sights of the town, the "must see" places. I really appreciated that and smiled while they chatted up their town.

"So this place. It looks old," I nonchalantly commented. The bartender looked up and nodded. "Do you have any ghosts here?" I questioned, not making eye contact, and continued on with my dinner. There was an awkward moment of silence. I lifted my eyes, looking directly into hers, and smiled. I think my freckles gave me a "you can trust me" face.

"Yeah," she said quietly. "I've seen things here. Mainly upstairs, late at night after we're closed. But yeah... I've seen things."

I could tell she did not want to discuss it further, so I nodded. I felt she was partially surprised yet partially relieved that I did not press the question any further. Not everyone believes in ghosts and spirits, even when they live in one of the most haunted towns in the country.

I settled my bill and thanked the bartender for keeping me company and returned to the hotel. The temperature had dropped even more, and I was thankful I had not walked the few blocks. The owner was inside and discussing a project on the phone. I walked away in order to give him privacy, yet stayed in his line of sight. When he finished his conversation, he walked over to me and asked how things were going.

"Great!" I said. "Do you have time to show me the videos you were talking about? I just need to run upstairs, put my stuff up. I can be back in a flash."

"Oh, sure! Come back down when you're ready. We can watch a few," he said.

"Cool. I'll be right back," I said and turned to go upstairs. This was going to be fun. Nothing like going to "ground zero" to get the inside scoop on the activity in the hotel. *I don't know how it can possibly be ANY better than what I've already experienced.*

Smiling that Cheshire cat grin, I returned to Room 19, excited to see video evidence of what had accidentally been caught on camera. I put the key into the lock and turned it to the left and entered a night I would never forget.

CHAPTER 8

❦

THE VALIDATION OF VICTORIA

Grabbing my nice arctically chilled Diet Coke, I headed downstairs. Creak, creak, creak. *There's no sneaking around this place. Note to self, no walking around late at night. I don't want to disturb anyone, and well, it's gonna be too cold anyway,* I thought as I closed the door to the room. At times, I am such a Southerner. If the temperature drops below 70°, I am bundled in layers. The low was expected to be in the lower 30s that evening, just above freezing, which meant only one thing to me - once I warmed up, I would not be moving until the "thaw" of dawn.

Walking into the Crystal Palace Ballroom, I stopped for a moment, overwhelmed by the brightness and the dazzling chandelier in the center of the room. Once my eyes readjusted, I was able to see the owner sitting over by the bar. There was a large screen against the wall, and the owner was readying for the paranormal show-and-tell he had promised.

"Hey there," I said, making my way back into the darkness. "Thanks for showing these to me."

"Absolutely! How's your stay been so far?" he asked, continuing to flip through the settings on the screen.

"Ohmergawd," I sputtered, instantly turning into a clone of a San Fernando Valley Girl. "It's been crazy! Do you want to hear about it? Or are you tired of hearing things like this?"

"Oh, sure, go ahead. I love hearing the stories," he said nonchalantly.

Immediately, and quite enthusiastically, I began telling him my third-eye adventures and of Jenny, the first spirit I encountered. Jenny had showed herself to me as a "tween", happy and playful, singing her name and playing with her dress. I told him she was really in my face and wanted to be seen. I realized I was speaking quite quickly, trying to get everything out before I forgot a detail, and I looked over to the owner. He had put the remote down and was no longer flipping through the channels on the big-screen television. Eyes opened wider, perhaps in astonishment, he looked at me.

"You know the room I showed you, the Pride Room?" he started.

I nodded yes.

"Remember how I told you there was a fire? And the owner's daughter died in the fire?"

Again, I nodded yes. I was beginning to feel like an

Opening Day Bobblehead Giveaway, free with the purchase of a full-priced adult admission. I smiled, hoping to indicate that I was in step with his story.

"The little girl who died? Her name was Jenny... and we have her bed in the Pride Room," he said with a serious tone.

I stopped nodding my head. Making that Cheshire cat face again, I blinked a few times before saying anything. Showing no fear, I said slowly, "Well... she's over in my room now. Guess she just wanted to say hi. She seemed very nice." I always try to put a pleasant and matter-of-fact spin on things. You never know when you might run into a lion, Androclus. It pays to be nice. The owner chuckled quietly to himself.

Internally, I was dancing around, spiking not a football but an orb of energy and high-fiving myself, alone in the paranormal end zone. "Psychic Score" I was screaming to myself. On the outside, I was smiling and very calm.

"Well, I have a message for you too, if you want it. From the lady in Room 19." I smiled at the owner. He nodded, giving me the green light to deliver the message. "She said she doesn't like being called the 'Jilted Bride' all the time. She acknowledges that is her lot in life, no pun intended, and she will be forever known as that, but it really hurts her feelings. It keeps bringing up the pain."

The owner nodded, understanding what I was alluding to. "She gets it, so I asked her 'what if we did something', just to let her know that we understand and care. She seemed open to that idea, so I told her I'd mention it to you."

He looked at me and accepted the fact that I had a conversation with the Bride of Room 19. It was nice seeing someone who was open and actually listening to me, not looking at me as if I were a bit off my rocker. "I was thinking," I started, "it might be something nice to do, and it could add to the atmosphere of the room without taking anything away. What if you made some sort of bridal bouquet of dried flowers and put them on the side table near the bed? You could let her know that they were for her and that she's not forgotten, and it would still look in theme with the Bridal Room." The owner nodded and understood the sentiment behind the suggestion.

"Oh, and there was a man I saw earlier too," I said, tapping my forehead and indicating I had seen him with my third eye.

"A man? What did he look like?" the owner asked inquisitively.

"He was at the other end of the hall," I began to tell him. I closed my eyes so I could recall the details. "He was standing at the bottom of the other staircase, you know, the one that goes up to the next floor. He had one foot on the bottom step, one hand on the railing. I had the feeling he was going upstairs, but stopped to look at me. He was leaning over, looking down the hall at me. I guess he was trying to figure out who was at the other end. I wasn't scared or anything. He didn't feel threatening in any way. He was just... *looking*."

"Can you describe him?" he asked again.

"Oh, sure." I still had my eyes closed. Quickly I began to prattle his description, starting at the top and working my way down, describing exactly what I was seeing, as if I were speaking with a paranormal police sketch artist. "He was an older man, tall, probably six feet or so, kind of boney. He had silvery hair with some dark in it, kind of long and thin, slicked back and behind his ears. It was kind of dirty too. He was wearing a dark jacket, like one they would wear in a western. It was long and stopped at the back of his knees. It looked rather heavy too, a thicker jacket. He had a black vest on, buttoned, and a white shirt. He was wearing some sort of string tie too. It was a bit floppy and limp. Dark trousers and boots, one foot on the bottom step. He had his other arm bent, and over his arm he had another coat, like a winter coat. It was dark too. He had deep-set eyes and deep wrinkles that ran across his forehead and down his face. I don't think they were really laugh lines, if you know what I mean. His face was rather elongated, thin, with a slightly pointed chin and cheekbones that stood out. I can't tell if he has a goatee or something, but I feel like there's something there, around his lips. I just really can't see it. Oh, and he had a hat. It wasn't a cowboy type of hat. It wasn't an Abe Lincoln hat. It was somewhere in the middle of the two."

Satisfied that I had described all I could see of the man with the hat down the hall, I opened my eyes and smiled at the owner. I noticed he was not smiling, not in the least. In fact, his mouth was slightly open, and the color had left his face for a moment. Without blinking, he said to me, "I've seen him. *Twice.*"

"Really! That's cool. This is like a psychic quiz! Can we see what else I can pick up?" I said jokingly. "So this man with the hat. He stays down at the other end of the hall, right?"

"No. People see him all over. You know what happened to Spielberg when he was in Jefferson?" the owner asked.

Oh, okay, here we go, back to bobbleheading, I thought, shaking my head sideways this time as I made that Cheshire cat face again.

"Spielberg was here in the '70s, making some movie," he started.

I smiled and continued to nod. "I bet it was *Sugarland Express!*"

"Yeah, I think that was the name of it," he said. Four years in college, studying film production, was not wasted. My inner film nerd was pleased. I actually knew the answer to "Name the Movie"!

"Well, when he was here, Spielberg and his crew stayed across the street at the Excelsior," he continued. I smiled and nodded, pretending to know what the Excelsior was. "One night, in the middle of the night, about two a.m. Spielberg wakes up and sees this same man in his room. He was so shaken, he jumped up and made everyone on his crew wake up, pack, and they left the hotel in the middle of the night! Spielberg and his crew even left the city and found another hotel, about twenty miles away. The entire crew was so tired and exhausted after working all day long, and, well, let's just say the crew wasn't very happy the next day."

The owner paused for a moment. Something outside in the hall caught his eye for a second, but he dismissed it quickly and continued on with his story. "This hat man left a lasting impression on him too. He even wrote him into *Poltergeist*. Yeah, the scary preacher guy is based on him!"

"Really! Wow! How cool is that!" I said. I did not want to tell him I did not exactly remember *Poltergeist* or the characters in the film. Of course, everyone remembers Carol Anne, but that was the extent of my *Polter*-knowledge. When the owner walked away for a moment, I whipped the phone out of my back pocket, did a quick Google search, and began looking for the scary preacher hat man from the movie *Poltergeist*. It only took a moment, and I found a still from the movie.

"What!" I gasped. I did a double take, not believing what I saw. Tapping on the phone like a crazed woodpecker and trying to make the photo larger, I stared at the screen for a moment, almost losing my breath. I reached behind me, waving my hand wildly, and searched for the chair. Never taking my eyes off the phone screen, I sat down slowly. The face that I saw on my phone screen... the face from the movie *Poltergeist 2*... the character Spielberg named *Reverend Henry Kane*... was the same man I'd seen earlier standing at the end of the hall, leaning around the banister and looking at me!

Scary Hat Man at Jefferson Hotel

So just who is the mysterious man seen throughout Jefferson? Very little is known about the man in the hat, who he might be, but numerous witnesses and reports through the years have described him as a tall male figure in a long coat and high boots. He makes no threatening moves; he just watches and observes. He just *watches*. Is he one of *The Watchers?*

Some guests have said they found it rather unsettling when they found him sitting or standing in their rooms throughout the night. Steven Spielberg would fall into this category. When I encountered the man the first time, I could only see him from a distance. He did not seem threatening, rather curious as to who was at the other end of the hall.

Whoever he is, he is apparently one of Jefferson's most solid and hard-to-miss ghostly apparitions. Several of the hotel's guests have reported following the man down the hall, thinking he was another guest, only to watch him as he turns and passes silently through the velvet ropes that safeguard the open doors, vanishing into the room.

CHAPTER 9

SEQUESTERED

I guess my poker face was not as good as I remembered. The owner recognized I had a few questions and was kind enough to let me rapid-fire them. My first question - *the water? Where is all the water? I know there's water around, I can feel it, feel the dampness in the air, but I just can't see it. That doesn't make sense.*

Much to my surprise, I found that the hotel originally sat at the edge of the bayou, back in the cotton days. What is currently the front of the hotel was originally designed to be the back of the cotton warehouse; the back was the front and later turned into the Jefferson Hotel.

If the building is at the edge of the water, then how was I able to drive down the street behind the hotel? There were even cars parked back there.

The large black metal doors, which roll up, were designed to be the front of the Jefferson, opening up to the bayou. That facilitated the loading and unloading of cotton. In fact, many of the buildings along the bayou had their entrances facing the waterway. After the water was redirected and the steamboat traffic ceased, entrances were reconstructed and now face the streets.

Shortly after the Civil War ended, railroad tycoon and now resident spiritual entity, Jay Gould appeared on the scene and wanted to put his railroad through the sleepy town of Jefferson. Much to his surprise, Gould was not given permission and left defeated. But, as all good ghost stories go, Gould did not leave before cursing the town. Thinking he had the upper hand in the matter, Gould managed to ensure the Texas and Pacific Railroad circled the outskirts of the town, taking jobs and the fortunes of the railroads with it. With the rerouting of the tracks, freight rates increased sky-high for the little town. Shortly after the deviation and loss of the freight line, the United States government removed the natural dam that backed the water up to the edge of the hotel. The water levels dropped considerably and made the Big Cypress Bayou and the lakes unable to be navigated.

AHA! I shouted to myself. I KNEW there was water here. It's just too bad... I mean, I picked up on it... I was just 150 years too late. At least I didn't drive off into the water in the middle of the night. Yeah, into water that is no longer there...

The owner continued to tell me small stories of the history of the hotel, never touching upon the paranormal tales from his own experiences and those of the other guests. One story in particular was equal parts of heartache and horror and again involved the most active room in the building, Room 19. During the hotel's heyday as an establishment for adult entertainment, one poor girl lost her life in the claw-foot bathtub that still resides in the room.

"People have reported hearing splashing in the bathroom," he began, "and when they go in there, flip on the light, there is no water in the tub at all. It's bone dry."

"Good to know," I said. "I'll make sure to take a quick shower and not linger in there." I had been planning on taking a nice long soak in the old cast-iron tub, but after hearing she died in it, I thought there was no reason to chance fate. Besides, you never know when you might need to make a quick dash out of the room. I thought it would be best to play it safe and stay dressed... *just in case.*

Feeling more assured and knowing that I would not be walking into a black abyss of liquid death, I took my leave and decided to return to the Bride's Room. *Creak, creak, creak. Man, these boards. You don't really need a security system. You can be heard walking down the hall. Hmmm, but do ghosts walk? Don't they just glide or hover, making no sounds?*

At last I made it down to the end of the hall, turning at the sarcophagus on the left. I greeted the room as I opened the door. "Hello, Room 19, I'm back! Did you miss me?" I was not exactly sure to whom I was speaking. Was I speaking to the ghosts in the hall, in the room or to myself? Maybe Jenny was back in the Pride Room and could overhear me. This is what living with a carnival of cats will do to a person. You just speak to anything and wait for a response. It always pays to be polite, too.

The hour was getting late; it was almost midnight. The road trip through time, history and the great state of Texas was quite long, and the experiences of the day were starting to show; fatigue was right around the corner.

Chocolate. Chocolate helps with the ghost hangover. Damnit, I should have gotten chocolate today. Oh well.

I continued on, chatting aloud for anyone who could hear me. There were no more messages coming through from the bride in the room, no sounds of Jenny singing and dancing. *Apparently you have a curfew or a bedtime even in the spiritual realm. Or maybe they were just exhausted too. How does all this work? I mean, the current "theory" is that those in the spirit dimension require energy to manifest, so they appropriate the energy of individuals who are around. What do they do when there is no one around? Do they run on half-life? No pun intended, of course.*

Deciding this would be the perfect time to tell those who were surrounding me goodnight, I wished everyone a pleasant evening and said I would speak with them in the morning. There was a calmness that came over the room, almost a feeling of acceptance. I took a few moments for quiet contemplation and envisioned a barrier of white light surrounding the room. As I do with every investigation and, frankly, every night before closing my eyes, I requested that only those who had the intentions of love and above would be able to enter the room while I was here. Shifting my personal resonance into a higher, more protected energy, I grew satisfied and felt completely protected and safe. Finding extra pillows in the cabinet (and have we not learned, I always look in the cabinet), I propped myself up against the headboard and pulled the blanket up to my chest. My security blanket, keeping the cold and spirits at bay.

It was difficult to comprehend. So many women had died in this area, in this tiny footprint of the Jefferson Hotel. Perhaps talking to them in the way I did helped a small bit, eased the pain, and allowed the room and the residential energies here to calm. A fragment of forgiveness. Perhaps letting them know that they were still remembered. I chose to remember them all as strong and independent loving women, facing life with broken hearts, abandoned and left with no other alternative, at times forced into a profession or decisions not of their choosing. When one finds themself faced with limited opportunities, circumstances often drive their hands to do things one never thought possible. It is a survival mode, the brain trying to cope and working in ways we never dreamt.

Settling back and getting comfortable, I began to drift off to sleep. It felt a bit odd, being able to look up, imagining that someone took their own life just above my head. I thought about that for a moment and felt no energy coming from the headboard. I did not feel like anyone was in the room with me. The room and I were both at peace.

Standing at the threshold of sleep, I began drifting through a crystal twilight of dreams. The north winds outside the shuttered windows made the visions clear.

Stars in the frigid night air shone brightly, the purity of the white light. Foreign pinpoints of lights guided me, so far away. I drifted, moving toward the distant twinkling lights, and slowly began to leave my body. I could hear myself breathing; I listened to sounds around me and the sounds outside, down in the alley below. A car drove down the street, the wind blew a bit stronger, and silence returned once again. No sounds were coming from the hall or any other rooms near me. As far as I could tell, the entire town had gently drifted to sleep.

Unfortunately, that peacefulness lasted only for a few moments. *Chug, chug, chug.* The Train from Hell was passing by, sounding its whistle. Loud enough to wake the dead. I immediately returned to my body. *No wonder this place is haunted*, I thought and chuckled to myself, still trying to remain in the zen state of sleep. Within a moment or two, the sounds of the train drifted down the tracks, taking my state of consciousness with it. Sleep was beginning to return. I could hear myself breathing again, relaxing with each breath. Rising up and out of my body and into the astral realities of another dimension. Breathing. In and out. Deeper and deeper, Relaxing, in and out.

It only seemed like a moment, but in the land of altered consciousness there is no way to measure time. *Chug, chug, chug, WHISTLE! Chug, chug, chug, WHISTLE!* After a moment or two, the train drifted off, taking the clanking and chugging with it.

And take that damn whistle with you too!

Settling back into my broken slumber, I began to drift

off again, this time a bit more agitated than the previous. I was confident I was still breathing, but I could not hear my breath. The ringing of the train was still echoing through my brain. Finally I found the quiet and the rhythm and began to fall back asleep.

Or so I thought.

The Train from Hell was doing more encores than Cher on her first Final World Tour. (I was lucky enough to see Cher on her first **and** second Final Tours. *Just how many "final tours" is one allotted? Inquiring minds...* I am not sure if she is still circumnavigating the Earth, looking for a place to land, or if she is still going.)

"Dear *GAWD!*" I said, sitting straight up in bed. *Does that go on all night long? Maybe THIS is why people run screaming out of the room! It's not a ghost that chases you out... It's the freakin' train! Does that damn thing go all night long?*

I reached for my laptop still on the bed. A quick Google search revealed my answer to the question *"do trains blow their whistles all night long".* To my chagrin, the answer was, *yes.*

Much like libraries and toddlers, there are Quiet Times and Quiet Zones. I began praying hard that I was in a Quiet Zone. *I guess I'll find out... in about forty minutes... when the 3:40 to Gawd Knows Where comes blazing through.*

So far, there was no ghostly or paranormal activity to report. Unless of course, that was a ghost train, and if that were true, then Shaggy and Scooby would not be far behind. *Maybe Freddie will drive us all down to the Malt*

Shoppe in the Mystery Machine. Oh, sweet Jeezus, I'm getting a bit sleep deprived.

I fluffed up the pillows behind my head, pulled up the blanket a bit more, and set off, trying to sleep again. I heard a gentle breeze of warm air blow through the vent above. *It must be getting colder outside. Well, that just means I won't run out of the building screaming in the middle of the night. I don't do the cold. No matter what happens, I'm staying here.*

At last, silence blanketed the town, the building and everything near. Peace was finally bestowed upon the sleepy community, and all was perfect in the world. *Wait? What is that noise? Oh, sweet Mother Mary!*

Chug, chug, chug, chug, chug.

I refused to open my eyes and acknowledge the train going by in the night. *No participant ribbon for you tonight, buck-o.* I waited for the whistle, but it never came. I looked at my watch. It was 3:40 a.m.! *Right on time,* I thought. And with that thought, the train and my consciousness drifted further down the line.

CHAPTER 10

❧

THE RETURN OF THE LIGHT

*F*or being a haunted and most murderous room, Room 19 was actually quite comfortable.

The daylight filtered in gently through the curtained windows, giving a soft glow to the room. It seemed I survived the night in the most haunted hotel in Texas. I stretched that "early morning sleepy" stretch, peeping out from under the blanket. It was cold out, and I only managed to get three or four hours of broken sleep. Checkout was not for several hours, so I decided to roll back over and try to take advantage of the time I had before my alarm went off.

I am not sure if it was the fact that I was away from the city or if it was the ambiance of the little town in Texas, but this morning made me think of visiting my family when they owned a farm. Mornings started early and quietly. I half expected to hear the sounds of the cows as they moved out into the pasture, or my dad walking out to the front porch and taking in the morning.

I knew if I made any sound, they would know I was awake, and I would be called to get dressed and help out. In these situations, I learned the value of remaining silent, and then I remembered I was in a town and not on a farm. From the other end of the hall, I could hear someone walking. The sounds of the steps were distant but familiar. There was almost a cadence to the footsteps. *Must be the owner checking everything out, making sure it's fine. That is the first thing I would do—the dawn patrol—walk the perimeter and get a lay of the land.* I was not sure why they would be coming down the hall. After all, I was the only one here. No one else had checked in for the night. It was just me and my ghostly gals… and one scary hat man!

The steps had a steady rhythm to them, never changing, never growing faster or slower. They were getting closer, and I began to hear the repetition clearer. *Step klump. Step klump. Step klump.* Whoever was walking down the hall had a limp. The steps began to grow louder, more intentional. They were getting closer to me. The creaking wooden floor grew louder, more pronounced, and began to echo in my room.

Jeezus, just how long IS that hall? It shouldn't take that long to get down to this end. It's a long hallway but not THAT long! The steps grew louder, echoing with more intensity inside Room 19. I could hear the footsteps echoing and bouncing through the room and through the bathroom of death. *If I were making a horror film,* I thought to myself, *this is*

EXACTLY how I would do it. Start out with something simple, like the bed shaking, and then move on to some form of sleep deprivation, psychologically gaslighting them the entire time.

Step klump. Step klump. Step KLUMP. Step KLUMP!

Hey-y-y-y-y! I continued thinking to myself. *Wasn't this the plot of the 1963 film* The Haunting, *starring up-and-coming Hollywood heartthrob Russ Tamblyn, who later went on to star in* Twin Peaks? *You know, that wasn't really a movie about a haunted house. It was a movie about a haunted person. The insane thoughts of Eleanor. Oh, geez, AM I ELEANOR?*

Cursing my brain filled with massive amounts of movie plots and trivia, I shook myself back into reality. There was an extra element to the footsteps now. I could hear that the *"klump"* step was a foot that was being dragged along. Like a midnight cowboy ready for two-stepping, I could hear the sound of sand beneath the foot. *It's easier to slide when there's sand on the dance floor.*

Louder it grew, keeping the same syncopation, the same boot-dragging sound, almost becoming deafening, crescendoing within my ears! *STEP KLUMP.* Echoing throughout the room and within my head! It was at my end of the hall. *STEP KLUMP. STEP KLUMP. STEP...*

Where the hell was the klump? Why was there no klump? There SHOULD be a KLUMP!

Propped up with pillows and leaning against the headboard, I rubbed my eyes in order to see clearly. I sat up, facing the door to Room 19. With only a lock on the door handle, I realized, the door was not really locked. If this was a true paranormal event, no lock would stop the door from flying open. The door, unique in design, was not original to the room. It appeared to be refurbished from another type of building and consequently did not fit tightly in the door frame. There was a gap between the door and the door facing, large enough to see shadows passing by. My room was still bathed in a gentle darkness, but the hallway was filled with the bright amber light from the window on the door at the end of the hall.

There was nothing but silence as I continued to look at the door. *I should just get up, go jerk that door open, and see who the Hell is outside the door,* I thought to myself.

Sanity came rushing back in as soon as I completed that thought. What would I do if there was someone outside my door? I was at the end of the hall, alone. No one would hear me if I needed help or screamed. I was waiting for the person outside the door to take another step, rattle the door, or make some type of noise. It was then I saw him through the large crack in the door. A large shadow. The shadow of what appeared to be a man, about six feet tall, swaying back and forth. I had the feeling he was trying to look through the crack, to sec if anyone was in the room. Instantly I was taken back to being a child on the farm. Make no sound. I pulled the blanket a bit higher, almost to my chin. The voices returned and told me to look at my watch and make note of the time. *Straight up 7 a.m. Remember this time. It's 7 a.m.*

I am NOT getting up. I'm not getting out of this bed. It's too early in the morning, and I'm tired. It's too early in the morning to see a scary shadow man. Besides, it's cold... and I don't DO the cold.

Was that the magical incantation needed to stop the swaying shadowy ghost? Was that all it really took? Or was the barrier of white light surrounding the room still holding strong? Was that why he could not see me? Was he being blinded by the barrier? Or were the spirits of Room 19 shielding me, keeping me safe from a shadowy man?

Whatever was projected appeared to work. The six-foot-tall shadow did not sway past the crack in the doorframe again. Feeling safe and secure and knowing that I had one hour left before the alarm went off, I snuggled down again for a bit more rest and fell into a magical deep sleep. I was exhausted.

Within the hour I woke, refreshed from my post-shadow-person nap. I gathered my things and packed my bags, deciding to leave, take a quick tour of the town, and return home. While I was packing, I began to play over the events of the early morning. I could not remember. What happened after the shadow stopped swaying? *I do not remember hearing anyone turn and walk back down the hall, but they had to walk back. Right?* I metaphorically scratched my head, trying hard to remember. The boards in the hall were quite loud. There was no way I could not have heard someone walking back down the hall... *unless they did not walk back...*

I packed and slowly began to face the morning. An hour had passed. Still wanting to see the town before I left, I decided to make an early exit and leave before the official checkout time. Trying to walk quietly down the hallway, I found that was an impossible task. The boards in the hall prevented any silent getaway. Taking one last look around as I walked downstairs, I smiled, thinking about the experiences of the past twenty-four hours. Once again, the little voices in my head did not let me down. They always guided me, this time directing me to take a trip that lifted my spirits, no pun intended.

I left the key to Room 19 on the counter, and not seeing the owners, I walked quietly to my car, loaded in my bags and ITC equipment (which I forgot to use) and drove around town. In typical fashion, I went down a road that I had not intended to take. The little voices were telling me, *Take a moment, go over the train track, and see what is on the other side. You never know when you'll be back here again.*

Seeing a large area that would make a great place to make a U-turn, I proceeded to drive forward. There was a small park that contained a car from an old railroad line and a statue of a Sasquatch. *A Sasquatch!?! That almost sounds like a T-shirt you would find on a weird paranormal vacation: "I went to a Haunted Town and all I saw was a Cryptid". I really am on the wrong side of the tracks.* I laughed to myself.

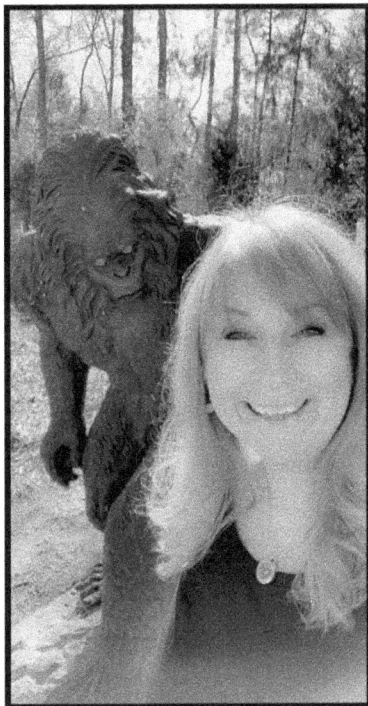

In addition to being the most haunted town in
Texas, Jefferson is also the American epicenter of
bigfoot sightings.

∾

*I*t has been my experience that road trips defy logic and time constraints. Taking a near-eternity to get someplace, it only takes half the time to return home. Apparently, there must be an increase in the gravity on the return trip, pulling us faster to our destination. Coupled with the fact my GPS led me down the back roads of Texas and through one wildfire, which allowed for the increased velocity, I began to feel a mathematical equation was in the works. *Everyone knows the first law of motion.* I felt Newton smiling down upon me, green-lighting my trip.

Feeling the jet lag from my little red car, I returned to the comfort and safety of my own paranormal house. After unloading the gear from the car, I sent a text to the owner thanking him for a wonderful time and asked, was anyone walking down the hall at 7 a.m.?

Within a few moments, the magical dancing dots reappeared, and a message soon followed. It was the owner. He said he was not sure, but he would check the security cameras in the hall and get back to me.

A few more moments passed, and the dancing dots reappeared. The owner sent a screenshot from his phone, showing photos of the cameras in the hall that faced Room 19. There were a few shots of people walking in the hall the night before, a photo of an empty hall, followed by a photo of me as I was leaving that morning. "No," he said. "It doesn't look like anyone was in the hall at 7 a.m."

Hmmmm, I thought, looking closer at the screenshot that he sent. Each photo was also time-stamped by the motion-activated security camera. *There HAD to be someone walking down the hall this morning. I know I didn't make this up. I know I'm not an Eleanor!*

I looked a bit closer at the screenshot, and then I saw it! Staring right at me!

The second photo from the motion security camera was time-stamped. The time stamp was 7 a.m.—the exact time I heard the shadowy person walking down the hall, stopping just outside the door of Room 19!

The video feed did not record anyone in the hall at that time, but then I remembered! The security cameras that lined the hallway... *are motion-activated cameras!* That could mean only ONE thing! Something was moving through the hallway. A moving object that was not photographed—something invisible! A moving object that triggered the motion-activated cameras to begin recording! There was an entity moving down the hallway at 7 a.m. that did not show up on the feed. *Was it possible? Could it have been an entity or a spirit? A ghost or a shadow person? A shadow person with a strong limp? Step KLUMP!*

And then, there it was. I felt the Cheshire cat grin creep across my face again.

CHAPTER 11

❧

SEPARATING FACT FROM LEGEND

*W*hat is the real history of Room 19? What happened in the room at the end of the hall, just to the left of the seven-foot sarcophagus? What is fact, what is fiction, and what is just local lore?

From what I witnessed, Room 19 is the hotspot of paranormal activity at the Jefferson Hotel. Thankfully, I did not know that at the time when I checked into the hotel. The room called to me, and I answered. I have always felt that reading up, studying and watching videos equates to a form of paranormal chicanery. I would much rather enter a room or area "cold", experiencing events on my own, and then later share my experiences. Hopefully there will be someone else who has shared the same experiences as I had. Validation can come from the most unlikely sources, sometimes.

Why is this room so haunted? Perhaps it is because of the anguish, a vibration from the pain of the heartache and of heartbreak, still echoing through time. The records of the hotel's lively history, especially in regard to the time the hotel served as a brothel, are understandably sparse at best.

One of the ghosts in Room 19 is a young woman trapped within the walls of the lavishly decorated room. I was told that a woman died in the cast-iron tub in the room, but I was not aware that she was a prostitute who was brutally attacked and stabbed one cold evening by a client, who left her to slowly bleed to death, dying in the claw-foot bathtub that still remains in the room. After purchasing the Jefferson, the most recent owners decided to research the room, trying to find and document any crime or murder that may have taken place in Room 19. After searching the local history and documents found in Jefferson, they were able to uncover a newspaper report about a young woman who was found dead in the claw-foot bathtub. She was reportedly stabbed multiple times, then placed in the tub, where she bled to death. Not saying a word about the stabbing, the man who paid for her company for the evening walked down the stairs, out the front door and disappeared into the mists of time. There was no arrest, no trial, no vindication for the woman who lost her life in Room 19. She tells her own story to anyone who will listen, even after death.

Evidence of the murdered young woman often appears in the mist and steam of the morning's hot showers. As if she was leaving a desperate plea for help, the name "Judy" is often found scrawled across the fogged mirror for others to see; other times words such as "help" will manifest on the steamed mirror, written by an unseen hand. Others have heard a frantic splashing in the middle of the night, the sound of someone drowning. Guests walk into the bathroom only to find the tub completely dry, no water to be seen.

From my own personal experience, I did not hear splashing in the tub; however there was perhaps a paranormal incident involving the toilet, which would not stop running. Somewhere between the 2:40 and the 3:40 a.m. Train From Hell, the toilet started running and filling up with water. Half awake, I staggered into the bathroom, jiggled the handle, and then proceeded to throw myself back onto the bed. After a few moments, I realized the toilet had not stopped filling up with water, so I returned to the scene of the crime (literally), jiggled the handle once more, and again returned to bed. The toilet continued to fill with water, and after a moment more, I returned to the bathroom, this time determined to stop the water from running. I removed the lid to the tank and saw that the flapper was seated correctly. There was no reason for water to still be running in the tank. *Ok. I get it. Bathroom. Water. Can we stop now, please?* I asked the invisible forces in the bathroom. I returned to bed for the third time. This time the water filled the tank and then stopped. Was the bathtub ghost hanging out in the tank of the toilet? Was this Judy's way of making her presence known? Or was this just an old toilet that continued to run in the middle of the night? I can hear the ghostly conversation now... *"Damnit, she's no fun. She doesn't get spooked."*

The most famous occupant of Room 19 has been described as a beautiful young woman. She most often appears to male guests who are traveling alone. Easily recognized, she wears a beautiful bridal gown, has long golden hair, and her feet... never touch the ground. When I found out this piece of paranormal trivia, I began to wonder if this was the reason the man left in the middle of the night earlier in the week.

Jefferson, Texas, is known to some as the "most haunted small town in the state of Texas". As many other guests have experienced, it is easy to hear whispers from nowhere, music from a closed dining hall, knocks on walls and headboards, phantom smells of cigars and perfume. Faucets turn on by unseen hands, doors pull back after they have been shut tightly, and gentle vibrations are felt as the train passes through the night. Children have been heard laughing and running throughout the creaking halls of the hotel in the middle of the night, forever free, living as exuberant children.

The Jefferson Hotel is a magnificent example of architecture and a spirit of time that has slowly passed. The current owners are wonderful people, stopping to share a ghost story or two as you sign in and go up to your room. One note of caution—it is elaborately decorated with rare and one-of-a-kind antiques, priceless items, ghosts, and definitely is not a place for children!

CHAPTER 12

✍

VOICES FROM THE FIELD

hat is a ghost?

It is a simple question and the first one I asked everyone I interviewed. I have to admit, it was fun to watch their faces when I asked that question. Instantly, everyone had a puzzled look. I do not think they were expecting something so easy yet so complicated. It is a question we have been asking since the dawn of time, since man first developed cognitive reasoning skills. Of the individuals I interviewed, the majority of the answers followed a similar thread, worded slightly differently based on an individual's religious and scientific backgrounds and beliefs.

Sifting through the answers, I found the thread. *What is a ghost?* It is, in the most basic form, *energy*. Nothing is ever proven in science, but there are theories that have large amounts of quantifiable evidence supporting them, the theories are considered "laws". One such law is the

"Law of Thermodynamics". The Conservation of Energy. Simply put, energy can neither be created or destroyed. It can only change forms. Following along with that line of thinking, if a person's perception is their reality, then their reality is based on their perception. Ergo, perception is based on the vibrational frequency of a personal resonance. In other words, if you are in the same vibrational frequency as Eeyore, then the world resonates in grays, negativity, gloom, and doom. Consequently, if someone happens to be living with seven small men in a tiny house deep in a forest and woodland animals can be conjured to do the housework, then one's personal harmonics is at a much lighter level. Imaginative and creative, beyond-the-box possibilities of the world can be seen without wearing the proverbial rose-colored glasses.

When I asked friend and best-selling author Teal L. Gray what her thoughts were on the incarnation of a ghost, she said, *"I think ghosts are remnants of the entities that have walked this Earth, whether that is the ghost of an animal, a human or other entities that have never been either. You know, they are something completely different, and I don't think a lot of other entities die, they just are transformed. We join into their transformation into another dimension after we pass. In that cross territory, even in inner-galactic travels, when we sleep, or even when we astral travel, we encounter them.*

"Are there people who are more predisposed to see ghosts? Good question. I equate it to how some people can play a musical instrument by ear. They can just pick up anything and just go. Then there are people who have to take lessons.

No matter how hard they try, no matter how gifted they are, they never flow or sound the same as someone who can play by ear. Some people work on it, and some people don't have to, they're just organically connected, and I think that's the difference.

"I grew up in haunted houses, and I think it was a natural thing for me to try to search for and understand what is going on, what is happening. What I did find was that in every religion, whether it is largely based or historically founded or 'loose, little offshoots', there are more connections than differences. The only difference is verbiage."

$\sim$

*N*ever a person to mince words, author, researcher and fellow former *Edge Of The Rabbit Hole* host Mike Ricksecker succinctly shared his theory on ghostly manifestations, consciousness and the afterlife when I posed the question. According to Mike Ricksecker:

"By the word 'ghost' you're talking about an Earthbound spirit in a non-corporeal form. I think there are different types of ghosts, and a lot of people try to really differentiate between a spirit and a ghost. What I believe is that a ghost is the manifestation of a human spirit that has passed.

"Scientists are now talking about how they believe in an afterlife. A scientific study recently released states that they believe that the consciousness goes off into the cosmos after death. Finally, they are admitting something we have been

talking about for the past thousand years. The body dies, but the consciousness remains.

"There is a belief out there that rather than the consciousness living within the body, the body is actually a receptor that the consciousness is being broadcast from elsewhere in the universe, in another dimension of the Ethereal plane, and is being broadcast down here to Earth and the body receives that 'signal'. When the body passes away, the consciousness returns to those origins."

While I have not heard this particular theory before, it would give credence to the reports of "walk-ins"* and, to a degree, the "Matrix Theory".

~

While interviewing several friends and colleagues, I began to notice a commonality between those of us who are seriously working and investigating in the paranormal community versus those who are wandering, locked in the darkness of mind and sight. I am ecstatic to say I see this as a growing trend, and I am optimistic that other researchers and experiencers in the paranormal world will be continuing in this direction. Researcher, author and inspirational speaker Morgan Knudsen summed it up perfectly when she dubbed it *"the joyful side of the paranormal"*.

"It's a higher calling," starts Morgan, *"finding the joy in the paranormal. We are not running around screaming. We're really promoting a joyful side of the paranormal. There's a*

higher calling with this subject matter for everybody. I think it's a greater calling to understand Consciousness, where we are, where we come from, and who we are. As it is in life, in the paranormal world, your emotional wounds, along with your positivity, will manifest in your experiences. It is up to you to find the joy in the moment."

*A "walk-in" is the theory suggesting that a person whose original soul has departed the body, generally through trauma or intense and devastating personal problems, where the soul was looking for an "exit" and has been replaced with a new and generally more advanced soul. The "new" soul retains the memories of the host body. The personality, abilities, and "life mission" of the host body suddenly changes. The primary benefit of walking into an adult host body is that the more advanced soul is allowed to carry out its mission without having to go through the maturation that humans need to reach adulthood. Basically, a "walk-in" has a defined purpose and "skips" the twenty-plus years it takes to mature, providing the new soul a more expedient way to achieve a goal or a life path.

CHAPTER 13

MORE STORIES FROM JEFFERSON

*H*auntings in this town are not exclusive to the Jefferson Hotel. Extending beyond the shadowy, haunted buildings, most of the residents in Jefferson have had a paranormal experience. Many are eager to share their adventures and leapt at the opportunity to recall their paranormal experience to anyone who would listen.

Similar to myself, author Teal L. Gray has witnessed paranormal activity her entire life. To Teal, "the little things that go bump in the night" do not frighten her; they are simply another part of life. Taking time from a recent book promotion tour, Teal shared several stories of her otherworldly encounters from a few of her trips to Jefferson.

"The Ruth Lester House was built in 1860," begins Teal, *"and in 1869 the house was sold to the Immaculate Conception Church—so there were nuns running it."* Teal chuckled lightly

at that thought. I knew instantly that this would be another great example of the *"joyful side of the paranormal"*.

"The house changed many times," she continued. *"It was a convent and a hospital, also Saint Mary's Private School. Later it was home to the Rabbi of the Hebrew Congregation. There have been many incarnations of that home, and along the way, masses of people were intermingling, living, and dying there. It was really interesting when I stayed there. They normally don't rent it out, but they knew me, and I also had two friends with me. I stayed in the main bedroom. My two friends were across the hall in a room that has twin beds. It's still set up that way; it's a beautiful home.*

"When you walk up the steps, and you don't even have to be psychic, you just feel like you're not walking into somebody's house. You feel the crowds there.

"It had been a really long day, and we were all tired. We ended up going in and getting ready for bed, and I left the light on at the stairs, just because we were in a new place, and I didn't want my friends to forget that there are stairs. I left that one on, but I turned off the one that is in the hallway that joins the two bedrooms. I turned that light off because of the way the light was shining. It was going more through their door. They kept saying the light was keeping them awake, and they asked if I could turn it off. I told them, 'I just thought it was safer,' so I left the stair light on, and I absolutely, on purpose, turned off the other hall light.

"It's beautiful, but it just felt creepy from the get-go, even in the daylight. There's a little rocker at the end with a little table, and I'm sure that that's probably where somebody would be

*stationed. It was a nunnery at one time, and I'm sure someone was stationed there, keeping all the girls aligned, keeping everybody in their beds. It just felt like someone was **stationed** there.*

*"I didn't think about it, and I turned the light off, went to bed, and a few minutes later, the light came on. I got up quickly, not because I was scared, but because I thought the people with me needed something. I got up, and I didn't see them, so I knocked on their door, thinking they might have needed something. I actually woke them up, so no, it wasn't them. They shut their door and went back to sleep, and I turned the light out and went back to bed. But this happened two more times. I guess there was someone down there who didn't want me to make them sit in the dark. It wasn't my place; and besides, they were the ones running the show, so they were like 'who are you to turn out the light, **this is the nunnery!**'"* Teal laughed again, thinking about turning the light off so many times and leaving the invisible guard in the dark.

"It was in the wee hours of the morning. I was finally tired from going back and forth and turning off the light. I just left it on, and they didn't say anything, so I thought, they're asleep, and they don't even know if the light is on or off. I went into what I thought was a pretty deep sleep, and then I heard something. I don't know how many times it repeated itself because I heard it several times in order to wake me up. I thought it was at the door, but in my mind it didn't sound like a knock on the door, but it was a repetitive sound.

"I opened the door, and I couldn't believe it for a minute. There was an old woman in a nunnery uniform sitting in the rocker, and one of the back legs was going 'bump, bump, bump'

against the back wall. I was thinking, 'Is she going to interact; is she a residual spirit?' And then she turned and looked right at me. She was an interactive spirit! She didn't speak to me, she didn't say anything to me, but when she turned and looked at me, she stopped rocking. It was just a few seconds, and then she was gone."

~

"**W**hy is Jefferson so haunted? Oh, I have no idea," begins paranormal enthusiast and experiencer Bobby Godwin. *"I have no idea, but you can feel the energy when you step foot in that town. When I pull into Jefferson, I can just feel the vibration of the land. I can just walk the town and just feel it—energy coming from the buildings, coming from the ground.*

"The very first time I went to Jefferson, I went with my son. The Jefferson Hotel was not open yet, it had just been purchased by the new owners, and they were getting it ready for opening. My son and I stayed across the street at the Kahn Hotel. We stayed upstairs, in the very last room, and brought balls for the little spirit of the little boy that resides there. I told him, 'Hey, if you want to play with these balls, they are here. You can play with them." We left and went on the Ghost Walk, and later that evening when we came back, the balls had been moved all around the floor. I didn't see them move, I wasn't there, but when we got back, they were all over the room.

"The first time I stayed at the Jefferson Hotel, I was there by myself, and I stayed in the train room, where there are reports of

a little red-haired boy spirit in that room. I have a train set that I built for a little boy named Ryan, and that's why I wanted to stay in the train room. I put the train cars out, all around, on the floor and on the counters, and I invited the boy who is said to live in that room to play with the trains. He's more than welcome to play with them. I explained to him that I like to play with trains. I have my own train set. I even pulled up pictures on my phone of the train set I was making, which was in progress at the time.

"Nothing was happening while I was actually in the room, so I decided to leave for a bit. I walked around, checking out the town. When I came back to the room, I unlocked the door, and when I walked in, I noticed that my toothbrush and a few other things were thrown on the floor; the restroom was in disarray. It was like someone came in and just wiped everything off the counter and threw it on the floor. The train cars were all moved around too. I called down to the owner and asked if anyone had been in my room while I was out. He said no, housekeeping doesn't normally clean the room until the person checks out. I told him ok and then mentioned to him my toothbrush and a few other things were on the floor and the train cars were all moved around the room. The owner said that the trains moving by themselves was a common report, and he had even seen that himself. The second time I went, I took a train car from my personal collection. When I went upstairs, the door was open, so I left one of my train cars there inside the room. I told the little red-haired boy that he could have it and play with the train car. I told him, 'I am gifting it to you.'

"The next time I stayed there, I went to Jefferson for History,

Haunts, and Legends, and I stayed in the Bride's Room. It was right after I got my first Covid vaccination, and as I was driving to Jefferson, I could feel it. I was getting sicker and sicker. I was meeting a group of friends there, some of us were on the top floor, some of us were on the bottom floor, and when I got out of the car, two of my friends told me, 'You look like crap.' It was hitting me hard, and I told them, 'Thanks. I feel like crap. I need to go and lie down.' I went upstairs to the Bride's Room and crawled into bed, and I literally passed out. I had a fever, the shakes; I had everything that some people experienced with the first Covid shot.

"I was lying in the middle of the bed on my side, and I felt the bed begin to rock. It stirred me out of my slumber, and I felt the bed push, which made me roll over to my back. I instantly jerked up in bed, and I looked to my left, and I saw the mattress rising up! It looked like someone was standing there and pushing the bed. It was amazing because my fever had broken; I was feeling so much better. It felt like the energy that was there, whoever was there... whether it was the bride or the young lady who had been murdered in the bathtub... or even a combination of the two, I felt like they were looking out for me, they took care of me, and when they felt like my fever was gone, they said, 'Ok, let's wake him up,' and that's when they lifted the mattress. I got up and said, 'Thank you for the wake-up call.'

"I went downstairs, and I started talking to the owner and told him what happened. The owner said, 'Really!' and confirmed that the bed has been reported to have been pushed and shaken while people are in it.

"It was really an amazing experience. It felt like a nurturing, caring spirit taking care of me."

I was extremely excited to hear Bobby tell his story, once again reaffirming that there is a gentleness to the paranormal world, and it is nothing like what is portrayed in "paranormal entertainment television". With the majority of the population blindly believing what is seen in the media, not taking the years that would be required to read, study and research this field, I feel that "paranormal entertainment television" is actually doing a disservice to the comprehension and understanding of what a true paranormal realm is. As Morgan Knudsen said, *"The science is behind what we're talking about and supports us completely. We just need for the world to see that."*

∽

Long before owning the historic and haunted Olde Park Hotel in Ballinger, Texas, author Dan LaFave spent decades investigating, experiencing, and living the paranormal life. There is a special breed of investigator who visits Jefferson for the first time, only to discover they have been "infected" with the haunted nature of the town. There is no fighting it; we return time and time again. Dan LaFave is no different. The history and elegance of a time long gone instantly captivated him. Dan, like so many of us, was drawn in, returning often to explore and experience the hauntings within the historic Jefferson Hotel.

Several of his favorite experiences and ghostly encounters stem from a time when he was a solo investigator over thirty years ago. One of his most treasured encounters came from none other than the ever infamous, Room 19. Here, in Dan's own words, are the events that took place one night in the historic and haunted Jefferson Hotel.

"I couldn't wait to stay in Room 19! I'd stayed in a few of the other rooms, so I went to Jefferson during the middle of the week. The hotel was about half full that night. I remember there was a group about two doors down from me. The way they did things back then is they would let groups book in, and they would have all sorts of groups going and doing things in the building. Some of them were a little noisy. I was sitting in Room 19, waiting for things to happen.

"At the time, they had a journal you could borrow, sit down and read other people's stories. You just had to turn the journal back in when you were finished. I was sitting in my room, reading that, trying to find out any additional things I could find out about the Jefferson.

"As the night went on, these groups got really loud and kept running up to my door, knocking on the door, and then running off. Finally I decided I needed to go out in the hall and say something—they're driving me nuts!" Dan chuckled to himself. There was a twinkle in his eye, and you can tell, it is in his blood too.

"I remember getting up and walking over to the door and just casually opening it. There on the other side were two younger girls listening and trying to hear if anything was going

on in Room 19. I guess they didn't know anyone was in the room, and when I opened the door, it scared them, and they almost jumped out of their skins." Dan laughs a little bit harder at that memory.

"Then they asked me, 'Can we come in, can we come in and just look at the room?' and I told them, 'Sure, nothing was really happening.' So they come in and do their thing and then leave. I kept reading the journal. There were some entries about Room 19, and one of the things that popped up was a story about the mirror in the bathroom.

"The way they described it was that if you go into the bathroom and close the door, then turn on the tub and run the hot water, it will steam up the room and fog the mirror, and you will be able to see writing on the mirror. Many of the times, the writing would say 'Help Me'.

"Now the curiosity is really starting to get to me, and I thought, I need to go in there and start running experiments. I go into the bathroom and followed the instructions, closed the door, and go back to sitting in the rocking chair and reading more in the journal. I waited about five minutes; I could even see the steam coming from under the door, so I got up and go in there. Of course, the bathroom is all steamy, and I turn off the water in the tub and go look at the mirror, and there isn't a darn thing on the mirror. I think to myself, 'Great, it's just folklore.' I decided to give it one more try. I wiped off the mirror, let all the water out of the tub, let all the steam out. I decided to do it again.

"I go back to the chair and pick up the journal, and I start to listen. All of a sudden, I hear the bathtub valves being turned.

As they are turning, the water in the bathtub stops running. I'm sitting in the rocking chair, thinking 'what the heck'. The water stopped running. I'm staring at the door, and I finally get up, and I walk to the door, and I'm pretty apprehensive.

"This time, I open the door, and I look over to the bathtub. Sure enough, the water wasn't running. At all. As the steam is starting to come out of the bathroom, I keep looking. I'm transfixed on the tub, but then I turn and look at the mirror, and there is writing on the mirror. It looked like someone took their finger and wrote something really scribbly. I walk over to the mirror, and as I'm looking, sure enough, I see something that looks like 'Help Me' written on the mirror. It was at a weird angle, and I was just looking at it, going, 'What the heck?'

"So I literally get real close, put my eyes real close to the mirror, and I'm looking, and I start to wipe it off, and then I realize—there's some kind of residue on the mirror. And I start thinking somebody must have sprayed something on the mirror that is creating this effect. I can't even describe what it was; it was like a 'gunky residue'. I took my fingernail, and I began to scratch it, and as I scratched it, it went all over the mirror. It totally distorted the words. I couldn't see the words anymore. I kinda messed it up.

"I decided to take a piece of tissue, and I rubbed it, really rubbed it. A lot of that residue was coming off, and the rest of it was smeared. I was thinking, 'AHA! I finally caught them! Somebody is trying to trick me here.'

"I cleaned off the mirror, let the water out of the tub, and decided to try again. I let the water run for about five or ten minutes. This time, the bathtub did not turn off. I get up and *walk in there and turn off the bathtub, and when I look at the mirror, the writing is there again, exactly as it was before. All the scratching, all the messing up I did on the mirror—it's all gone! It's back to exactly the way it looked before. It just didn't make any sense to me.*

"I begin looking at the mirror, trying to rationalize it, trying to explain it and figure it out. If this is some type of trick, how can they be doing it? It literally looked like the same way it was written before, the same place on the mirror, the same scribbly handwriting. When I scratched it before, it should have been smeared. It should have been all messed up or not even appear.

"I'm trying to figure it out, so I wiped the mirror, and I wiped it again, and it smeared all over the mirror. I decided I'm gonna give it one more try. I let the water out of the bathtub, and you know, they would have been mad if they knew I was using up all their hot water.

"So I do it again. I turn on the hot water in the bathtub, close the bathroom door again, and I go back to the rocker, but this time, while I'm sitting in the rocking chair, I begin yelling at the bathroom door.

"I told the door, 'You're pretty good, but if you're really doing this, prove it to me, prove to me that something is going on here.'"

Dan continued to yell at the door, *"I'm not convinced that you are real!"*

"Then the bathtub shuts off. Again! I hear the faucets closing, and I begin to hear a woman humming. Then I hear what sounds like fingers hitting the water, like they are playing on the top of the water.

"I'm sitting in the rocking chair, and it sounds like someone is playing in the bathroom. I watched the closed door for about three or four minutes, just listening to someone on the other side playing in the water. I get up and open the door really fast, look straight at the bathtub, and there's not a darn thing there, just the hot water with steam coming up.

"I look at the tub, and then I look at the mirror. Again, across the mirror I can see 'Help Me', but this time, there is a third word scribbled underneath... and it's my name."

CHAPTER 14

❧

THE EXCELSIOR HOUSE HOTEL

*I*n addition to the Jefferson Hotel, the Excelsior House Hotel, located diagonally from the Jefferson Hotel, has its fair share of ghostly encounters. The Excelsior House, originally a nineteen-bedroom, mid-nineteenth-century roadside inn, is the second-oldest hotel in Texas and holds the distinction of being the oldest *continuously* operating hotel in the great state of Texas (the Menger Hotel, across the road from the Alamo, holds the honor of being the oldest hotel but has not been continuously operated). Located in the heart of Downtown Jefferson, the historic hotel has been welcoming travelers since 1858.

The Excelsior House Hotel was built by Captain William Perry. Perry, a native of the New England area, was among the first to guide a steamboat to Jefferson. He is also credited as the person who cleared the bayou, allowing for successful future riverboat traffic. Thanks in part to the boomtown explosion of Jefferson in the 1850s, the Excelsior House was expanded. In the 1860s, the Excelsior was enlarged to accommodate the growing population of Jefferson. Again in 2018, the hotel was renovated into the very bright and white building we see today. Wanting to maintain the elegance and grace that was found throughout the town of Jefferson, the original facade and design of the Excelsior House remained while the interior was updated and, to a degree, modernized. Proudly displaying a rather large Texas Historical Marker on the facade, the Excelsior House was declared a Historical Site, and in 1969, 111 years after first opening its doors, the Excelsior House was given a special honor and now lives forever in the National Register of Historic Places.

As with the majority of the buildings and homes in Jefferson, several reports of shadowy figures fill the haunted walls of the Excelsior House and have become intertwined with the haunted history of Jefferson. Numerous guests have reported disembodied phantom smells. Spectral memories of cigars and expensive Parisian perfume drift silently, haunting the hallways. As with most historic and haunted hotels, reports have been made of otherworldly figures drifting through the Excelsior Hotel: headless figures; children who cannot be seen run, laughing, throughout the building; mysterious women seductively and leisurely walk down the halls and slowly vanish into the unknown. Eyewitnesses have recounted the tales of a Lady in a Black Dress on several occasions.

When I hear stories such as this, I always find myself wondering... if given a choice in the afterlife as to whether I would choose to be a mysterious Lady in White or a Lady in Black, I think I would choose to be the elusive Lady in Black. The Lady in Black always has an air of mystery about her, fulfilling an agenda only she is privy to, walking the earth long after she has gone as if searching for the one thing she never could find in life. I do appreciate the air of mystery mingled with a sense of sadness. Perhaps the vibration of sorrow and loss carries through the veil and into the quantum reality where the paranormal resides. I find that to be intriguing, and also, well, even in the afterlife, black is more slimming. A girl always has to be prepared.

Towns such as Jefferson have developed and evolved into a rich folklore. Buildings that have taken on their own personality, land that has seen historic battles and blood-shed. It is only natural that such a place would attract the curious along with the rich and famous of the time. Many stories live within the walls of the Excelsior House. Tales of love, passion, crime, and mysteries live long after their participants have passed. Within the elaborately decorated hotel, the cream of society and political figures of the time have stayed at the Excelsior. Within the registers are names etched in history such as poet and playwright Oscar Wilde (known for *The Picture of Dorian Gray*—a magnificent work of double entendre), director Stephen Spielberg, first lady of the United States Lady Bird Johnson, President Rutherford B. Hayes, and a not too distant relative of mine, President Ulysses S. Grant. Though many of elite socialites, powerful businessmen and ruling families of the day such as John Jacob Astor and W. E. Vanderbilt stayed at the Excelsior House, none could compare to railroad tycoon Jay Gould.

On the second floor of the Excelsior, a large wooden door guards the "Jay Gould Room". As you remember, Gould was an American railroad magnate who wanted to run his railroad through the center of Jefferson. The citizens of the town decided against that, and feeling vindictive, Gould decided to circumnavigate his railroad around Jefferson, thus beginning the end of a financially thriving town. Many of the stories from the Excelsior House involve Jay Gould in some form or fashion. The room still has a distinct feel of the power that was wielded from inside, power that determined the fates of so many who lived in the area. He was called heartless by many and practiced unscrupulous business behaviors. A very harsh and stern man, the room named after him reflects that part of his persona. Furnished in harsh browns and golds with heavy walnut furniture dating from the earliest days of Jefferson, this room is fit for a railroad robber baron. Yet within this room, near the corner, sits an item evoking a sense of nostalgia, much softer in nature. A piece of furniture that fills the corner of the room with peace and comfort. Within the Jay Gould room is—a rocking chair with red velveteen cushions. *Not exactly the thing one would think of when you imagine a heartless businessman ruling from afar. I had to ask myself, would a man filled with cruelty such as Jay Gould return to a room, placate himself with nostalgia and sit in a rocking chair, playing puppet master and determining the fate of thousands who at that time called Jefferson "home"?*

One story that originates at the Excelsior is the story of a single mother who worked in the hotel. Having no other alternative, the young woman was forced to bring her child with her to work. Telling her son to be good, to be quiet, she left him in the unoccupied Jay Gould Room while she was cleaning another room in the area. While changing the linens nearby, her son ran in and insisted that she return to the room with him. Knowing that she would not be able to finish her work until she agreed, she quickly turned and followed her son. When they were both in the room, her son pointed to the rocking chair in the corner. *"Look, Mom. Look! The chair is moving on its own!"* Not believing what she was witnessing, she thought it must be a type of trick. Walking slowly over to the corner chair, she began to examine the rocker, making sure there were no strings or devices that would make the chair rock on its own. After a few moments and a careful examination of the chair and the corner of the room, she concluded that there was nothing attached to the rocker, nothing of this world controlling it. It was moving on its own.

Other shadowy figures have been seen haunting the hallways and courtyards of the Excelsior House. From the Excelsior's enclosed square, a mysterious figure has appeared and has been seen wandering up the stairway and down the hall. Many women traveling alone have told countless tales of being unexplainably woken from a sound night's sleep, only to find a mysterious man in black standing at the foot of their bed. Watching them sleep. *Just watching.*

Several individuals feel that this is the spirit of Abraham Rothschild, the extremely notorious and charismatic ladies' man with golden hair. In the late 1800s, Rothschild was a frequent visitor to Jefferson, traveling from Ohio to Texas on several occasions, working as a jewelry dealer and traveling salesman for his father's successful Ohio jewelry store. However, Rothschild has claimed his place of infamy in Texas history. He is suspected of being involved in the murder of his wife, "Diamond" Bessie.

THE LEGEND OF "DIAMOND" BESSIE

According to the local legends of the town, "Bessie", whose real name was Annie Stone, was an extremely attractive young woman, with dark, shining hair and snowy, silvery skin. After Annie left her home in New York, she moved west. There were rumors of a failed relationship with an older man, and Bessie set off on a new adventure and a new life. Unfortunately, life was much harder than she imagined, and soon, she turned to prostitution. Not long after she arrived in Texas, Bessie was found in the woods outside of Jefferson. She had been killed by a single gunshot wound to the head. The alleged murderer was her husband, Abraham Rothschild, the son of one of the prominent families of the day. Occasionally, visitors to the Excelsior House have claimed to have encountered and had experiences with Bessie.

As a child, I remember the East Texas branch of my family making sarcastic remarks in regard to someone being dressed "fancy", as they would say. *"Why, she must be richer than Diamond Bessie."* I always imagined it was just a phrase, an East Texas cliché, if you will. Just a way to make a disparaging remark at the expense of someone else. Imagine my surprise when I discovered on my first trip to Jefferson that "Diamond" Bessie was not only a real person, but actually a notorious unsolved murder! With the annual production of what could easily be equated to as the *Texas version of the Salem Witch Trials*, the eclectic town of Jefferson produces an annual drama about the murder and trial of "Diamond" Bessie... and has done so *for the past sixty-eight years.* This performance, which takes place each spring, is derived from court transcripts, commemorating the unsolved murder and the local trial that took place in 1877. *Purchasing tickets for this drama, which takes place at the Jefferson Playhouse, in advance is strongly urged.*

THE SAGA OF STEVEN SPIELBERG

One of the most famous paranormal sightings belongs to none other than legendary director Steven Spielberg.

'Twas a dark and stormy night, a Monday night, back in the 1970s, when a young Steven Spielberg came rolling through town with his film crew. The crew and the budding director had been out all day, scouting locations for what would eventually become Spielberg's theatrical feature film directorial debut, *The Sugarland Express.* Days on set can be grueling, often more mentally taxing than physical. After a particularly long day, the crew and Spielberg decided to spend the night in the Excelsior House and take a well-deserved night off.

Spielberg, being the director of the unit, checked into room 215—also known as the Jay Gould Room. Spielberg has remarked that he walked into the room and looked around at the heavy walnut furniture and the harsh brown and gold decor of the room. He said that he felt "uneasy" when he surveyed the room, feeling the power and influence that emanated from room 215. Finally making peace with his room selection, he walked over and gently tossed his briefcase on to the carved rocking chair in the corner, the very chair that has a history of rocking on its own. Before he could make it across the room, Spielberg heard a sound behind him. *Ka-**THUD**.* Turning around slowly, the only thing out of place was his briefcase. The case was now on the floor, the rocking chair motionless. Had the chair thrown the briefcase out and onto the floor? Dismissing it as nothing but an accident, he turned and began to get ready for a night of relaxation and, hopefully, sleep.

Feeling as if someone was constantly watching him,

rest did not come easy to the new director that evening. Tossing through the night, Spielberg woke shortly before 2 a.m. to the feeling of an invisible hand on his shoulder. Someone was shaking him, trying to gently wake him from his broken sleep. He sat up in the darkness. There in his room, he saw a figure of a little boy asking if he wanted breakfast. Just past the ghostly child, Spielberg saw the empty rocking chair moving on its own. It was at this point of the night when Spielberg openly came to the conclusion—his room was haunted! The sight of this ghostly child severely frightened Spielberg, and without pausing for an instant, he roused his crew, demanding that everyone pack. They were leaving immediately. In the middle of the night, the crew of *The Sugarland Express* left the Excelsior House and drove twenty miles to the next town and checked into the first hotel they saw.

It's been reported that seeing the chair rocking on its own and a ghostly figure at the foot of his bed left a lasting impression on Steven Spielberg. There is another rumor that he also saw the ghost of a tall man wearing a long western duster jacket stopping at his knees, trousers tucked into his black boots. A string tie around his neck, his face was lined with deep wrinkles. Shortly after his stay in Jefferson, Spielberg wrote the screenplay for *Poltergeist*, and it has been reported that he based the character "Reverend" Henry Kane on the otherworldly figures he saw in the early morning hours at the Excelsior House Hotel.

I find it very interesting that "the cowboy", as he is

referred to, has been seen throughout the town of Jefferson. In fact, I saw him not once, but *twice* while I was staying across the street in the Jefferson Hotel. Knowing that this phantom figure roams the area, I wanted to find out more. *Just who was this cowboy?*

As you can imagine, details are sparse, but there are reports of a cowboy being shot and killed in the streets of Jefferson. Many believe that "the cowboy", the same entity I saw on my first trip, is the ghost of James Wardell Gorman, who was shot on Christmas Eve 1871. Gorman was shot in front of the Kahn Saloon, the building next door to the Excelsior House and directly across the street from the Jefferson Hotel. After being gunned down, Gorman was carried inside the Jefferson Hotel, where he died from his wounds.

I think that on my next trip to Jefferson, I owe it to myself to stay in the Excelsior and experience more of the paranormal playfulness that this town offers to those who choose to see.

CHAPTER 15

THE KAHN SALOON AND HOTEL

*D*irectly across the street from the Jefferson Hotel stands the Kahn Saloon and Hotel. Built in 1865, the Kahn Saloon has a violent yet colorful history. It has been repurposed several times, existing as the "premier" saloon and brothel during the early Wild West days of Jefferson. In 2016, the Kahn Saloon was restored and turned into the extremely haunted Kahn Hotel.

It is the characters of the past that give rise to the stories of today. One such story is a story of an extremely unlikely friendship of two men, Jesse Robinson and Bill Rose, friends only because they were both disliked in the community. "Bad seeds stick together," they thought, and the most unlikely friendship began.

One afternoon, Rose and Robinson found themselves in a heated argument about going to the Kahn Saloon and having a shot of whiskey. Robinson, who was not interested, did not want to go, but Rose insisted. There was no way that Rose would take no for an answer. The argument escalated, and the two began to argue over everything, as bad seeds often do. Before long, the two friends found they were no longer arguing over whiskey but had gotten to the heart of the matter and found themselves arguing over a woman who worked at the saloon. Rose was standing on one side of the street, yelling at Robinson, who was standing on the other. Rose pulled out his gun and began to wave it around, accidentally shooting Robinson, who in turn pulled out his gun and, with a more accurate aim, returned fire and killed Rose. Robinson and Rose, friends because of a bizarre set of circumstances, shot and killed each other, falling in the middle of the street in front of the Kahn Saloon and the Jefferson Hotel.

Neither man had friends or family, so the town of Jefferson was left with the responsibility of burying the two outlaws. Near their grave—*that's right, grave, singular* —stand two iron posts that are connected by a chain. It is how the town of Jefferson chose to immortalize the two friends. They are buried together, in the same casket, chained together. Obviously, being physically chained forever to the person who murdered you is reason enough for paranormal activity to occur. They can be found together for eternity at the old Oakwood Cemetery.

Also seen at the Kahn Hotel are former residents of Jefferson who tragically lost their lives. Jessica, a madam of the one-time brothel, and her seven-year-old son, Andrew, were murdered during a robbery upstairs. Both mother and child have been seen in the hallways on the second floor of the Kahn Hotel. Being a typical little boy, even in death, Andrew has been reported to play tricks on guests, often hiding or moving items in a room.

Today, many visitors to the Kahn Hotel describe the sensation of an invisible hand touching them or gently pulling their hair. Within their rooms, personal items are moved. Sounds of doors opening and closing on their own still echo throughout the building. Is this the ghost of Andrew still playing?

While many guests experience what is most likely the ghost of Andrew, others have reported seeing Jessica. Reports vary, but for the most part, she is seen wearing a white dress and standing at the top of the stairs, forever on watch and guarding the ladies of the Kahn Hotel.

CHAPTER 16

❧

THE RETURN TO JEFFERSON

*W*hy do we return to this most haunted town? What is the draw, the seduction? What is it about Jefferson, Texas, that makes it so uniquely different from all other haunted towns? Is Jefferson the physical embodiment of the ghostly lover we find ourselves craving, just one last kiss, just one last touch? Is this why we return time and time again?

Each person I spoke with had a different answer, however, one detail ran congruent—once you visit, it is in your blood. Jefferson is a paranormal airborne pathogen, spread from host to host. It is a supernatural yearning, a chance to experience one more encounter. Initially, you feel you have immunity, but soon you are captivated by the history, caught in the mystery and the lore of this tiny little town deep in Northeast Texas.

Hauntings and paranormal activity are not limited to the Jefferson Hotel. Activity of a ghostly nature is part of the subculture of Jefferson, Texas. Much like a residual haunting, one can perceive the energy of the paranormal by merely walking down the sidewalks of the downtown area. You are never alone; eyes are always watching you.

~

J admit it. After one visit to this tiny town, I found myself infected, and I was not searching for a "cure". I wanted to visit, return for a weekend, or just move here, but the logical mind always rains down on daydreams. I knew moving to Jefferson was not a reality for me. *At least, not yet. Never say never. Who knows what the future may hold? Oh, wait, I do in a way. I clearly see multiple timelines lying before me, and like the Fool at the start of a deck of tarot cards, I have one foot raised, just waiting to take a step on a new journey. I do not have a little dog at my heel; I have a cat. A most metaphysical and magical tuxedo cat. Maybe I am the Fool, standing shoeless on the edge of my future with my face turned to the warmth of the sun. Until it's time to put my foot down, I'll just stand here, wiggling my toes in the ether.*

A few months past my original visit to Jefferson, I attended a small paranormal event in North Texas. While at the event, a friend asked if I was going to "HHL" in November. I just looked at him, blank eyed, and sheepishly smiled.

"You *do* know about it, right?" he asked. I suddenly began to feel out of touch and unaware of the happenings of Northern Texas.

"Texas is a big state, and I'm in the Southeast part," I told him. "I'm not sure what happens up here. What is this 'HHL' you speak of?"

His eyes suddenly grew large, almost double in size, and the excitement rose in his face and in the tempo of his voice. I suddenly had a front-row seat for "the Edification of HHL".

"HHL" is what those in the know call the biannual event that takes place in Jefferson. "History, Haunts, and Legends" is a paranormal Shangri-La for the Texas paranormal enthusiast. A weekend event held in the spring and in the fall, the town of Jefferson becomes fully engaged in the paranormal world. It is a weekend of unimaginable celebration of "all things paranormal". I knew immediately this was a weekend event I must attend.

While the actual event is only one day, those of us in the paranormal community have managed to stretch it into a three-day weekend and descend upon the town (and for those of us who plan ahead, it is a four- or five-day weekend). When I made arrangements to purchase my tickets, I was asked to be a vendor for the event. I was extremely honored to be asked and immediately said yes. Perhaps the Fool is beginning to put his foot down. Maybe this was a first step deeper into the paranormal world. With that thought, I started to search for a bed and breakfast and began to plan my extended stay in Jefferson.

CHAPTER 17

❦

THE GIGGLING GHOST OF WHITE OAK MANOR

*I*f past experience has taught me anything, it is to go blind into a paranormal situation but do *not* go blind into your accommodations. *Seriously, who has an Airbnb in South Texas without air conditioning in the summer! Live and learn, I suppose.*

One of the most beautiful and attractive things in Jefferson are the historic homes that have now been turned into bed and breakfasts. Jefferson, previously known as the *Bed and Breakfast Capital of Texas*, was beginning to mesh my two loves together. *This is shaping up to be an interesting weekend.* I began my search and hoped to find a small BnB with perhaps a small ghostly presence too.

It is rather difficult to search for a haunted BnB while trying to avoid any description of who haunts the home. I found a charming home called White Oak Manor and accidentally saw the words "ghost of a girl". Everything happens for a reason, I suppose, so it must have been an intentional slip of my eye. For years, the spirits of children have been attracted to me. *It must be that "mom aura" I naturally radiate.* So many times I have found myself taking care of small children, small animals, and lost souls. If I were to meet an entity while alone in an unfamiliar town, I would rather it be a little girl.

Quickly I booked a room for one night before I was tempted to read any more about the alleged hauntings in the house. With the majority of the weekend activities happening in the historic section of town, I decided to arrive early, research the area and then move to the historic Jefferson Hotel later the next day. Jumping over to the next website, I saw the "Pride Room" was available. On my first visit to Jefferson, I had made contact with Jenny, the little girl who died in the fire of the original Pride Bed and Breakfast in 1901. *Let's just make it a little girl ghost weekend. See how many I can get in touch with.* I eagerly booked the room for the rest of the weekend, thinking that the Fool's foot was getting closer and closer to the ground. Soon, I would be off on my new journey.

~

*E*xcitement, along with a low-pressure cell, was building as I packed my bags. I loaded up my small car and eagerly set sail on my excursion to Jefferson.

How far away is Jefferson from home? Oh, it's about four hours. In Texas, we measure mileage not by a physical distance, rather we measure it in "hours". The actual distance via a road really has no bearing on a trip. I once lived thirty-five miles from Houston, yet it took over seventy minutes to drive the route. Hills, traffic, construction. They all play a part in the Texas roadway system. Four hours for a trip is not a huge trip for a native of the state. We take it all "in stride". In less than seventy-five songs from my shuffling iPod, I had arrived at my destination shortly before dark. I quickly unloaded my car, gathering my overnight bag and my ITC gear, and began to make my way to the manor.

The house was charming, a quaint two-story home with a wraparound porch, a swing off to one side, and surrounded by a white picket fence. I walked up to the gate and opened it and began walking up the pathway, noticing it was in the geographic center of the house. Stopping to take it all in, I set down my bags and straightened my back, looking up to the top of the house. In the center of the second floor was a window, also lined perfectly with the geographic center of the path. *Very nice, how symmetrical.* I continued looking up, and I noticed that in the center window there stood a man. He had pulled back the white sheers and was leaning against the side of the window. I only had a brief glimpse of the little man, but I could see that he was covering his mouth, his shoulders shaking, rising up and down. I blinked, hoping to get a better look at this little man in the too-large suit, but I was not able to. He had disappeared. *Rude. How* **rude!** *He's LAUGHING at me! I don't remember reading anything about this place having a giggling ghost. Well, if you're going to laugh* *at me, the least you can do is get down here and help me with my luggage. Giggling Ghost, indeed. This is how we're gonna play it? Ok, I saw you. I gots ya number. Well, at least I amused the ghost. Nothing scary here.* I snickered to myself, bending down to grab my bags again, making my way around the side of the house.

Walking around to the left side to the entrance, I stopped to put my bags on the steps and catch my breath. I straightened up again to stretch out my back, and standing before me on the porch was the little man. This time, I was able to get a better look at him.

He was small in stature, wearing a black suit that was way too large for him. I had the feeling he had passed quickly and unexpectedly, and at that time, any suit would do. The shoulders of the jacket extended about two inches from his body on both sides, the sleeves bunched up, and his trousers echoed the same. Obviously this suit belonged to someone who was about a foot taller than this little man on the porch. He was wearing a white shirt and, much like the man I had seen on my earlier trip to Jefferson, a string tie around his neck. He was wearing black glasses, clear-ish on the bottom of the frame. His hair was thinned and silver, slicked straight back on his head. He appeared to be sweating, his cheeks flushed with red. Again, he was covering his mouth and laughing at me with such fervor, his upper body was shaking. This time I saw he had a white handkerchief, like all true Southern gentlemen, balled in his hand.

I looked down at my bags. *Oh, so you came down to help*

me carry this inside? I looked up, and he was gone. *Ghosted by a ghost. That sounds like a Taylor Swift song. I think Mr. Giggles must like me or something. Why else does he keep showing up? And he was blushing too. Did I tickle Giggle's fancy? Still, he could help me with my bags. Rude.*

Grabbing everything from the steps, I made it the last few feet, punching in the code and finding my room. I walked in, setting my bags at the end of the bed. *Oh, wow. There's a fireplace in my room. I would love to live in a place like this. Wonder if I could come back and haunt here too?*

Thinking I was the only one in the house, I left the door to my room open and walked across the wooden floor to the yellow wingback chair. I did not feel alone. I looked around the room, hoping the ghost of the little girl was here, but the room did not feel like a little girl. It felt like something *different.*

I pulled out my dowsing rods and asked if I could ask a question. Without hesitation, the rods swung quickly into an X, indicating that the answer was a yes. *Wow, you guys never move that quickly at home. This town must be really charged. It's a good thing I wasn't leaning forward. With the speed of the rods, I could have poked myself in the eye.*

I asked the rods to return to a forward, neutral position. They quickly obliged. I giggled at the speed of their movements. *"The joyfulness of the paranormal."*

Can you tell me, did I see a little man standing in the top window? Quickly they returned to the X formation.

Oh-kay-y-y-y. Can you tell me, did I see a little man on the porch? Swoosh. Another X.

Alrighty, then. Return to neutral. The rods obeyed. *Is the little man here with me now?*

Without wasting a second, they swung back, indicating a strong yes.

Hmmm. Can you point to where he is in the room? Without missing a beat, the X was broken, and both dowsing rods pivoted and pointed to the open door to my room.

I have never had dowsing rods act so quickly before. It made me wonder, is the town of Jefferson really so charged with the energy of the paranormal? Or was this the energy of the Giggling Ghost? I could no longer see him, but you could feel him nearby.

*What? He's in the **doorway**?* The rods again answered yes.

"Ok, Mr. Ghost," I said aloud, extending my arm, palm facing the door. "Let's establish the rules. You are NOT allowed in my bedroom while I am here. And you CERTAINLY are not allowed in my bathroom. Nope, not at all. You are welcome to stay in the parlor if you like." I pointed to the parlor adjacent to my bedroom. "I'll be more than happy to talk to you out there, but in here, it's a no-go." And with that, I walked over to the door and kindly shut it, locking it from the inside. *Yeah, like a lock will stop a ghost.*

There was a different feeling to the room. A bit lighter, if you will, and I knew that he was gone. Knowing that a little girl was supposedly here, I removed my rings and bracelets and placed them on a coaster on a table near the window. Picking up my phone, I snapped a few photos. If she was going to play with them, I wanted to document their original positions.

Having my camera in hand, I thought I would take this time alone to walk around downstairs, shoot a bit of video for a friend of mine who could not make the trip with me. I went into the parlor and sat on a wonderful vintage settee. Looking at the fireplace in the room, I noticed that if you were to take the angle of the fireplace in my room and add it to the angle of the fireplace in the parlor, it made the beginnings of a triangle. I had seen fireplaces like this in other houses. It is a very clever design, that is, if they all share a chimney. I wondered if there was a fireplace in the room next to mine.

I began walking towards the hearth, shooting video as I started my tour and narrating my journey for my friend. Looking through my phone as I walked, I saw something gray swoop down and in front of me, stopping me in my tracks. I did not see it with my eye, but only through my phone. When I stepped back, my finger slipped from the record button, and the recording stopped. It almost looked like someone ran by in a gray cloak, someone who was about the same height as I am. Instantly, I thought of the cover of the old Scholastic book *The Witch Of Blackbird Pond*—a reading staple for any girl growing up in the South. *It's the gateway book to the WooWoo.* I started to record again, telling myself I would play it back later and check for the swooping gray cloak.

～

*T*he night passed quickly and peacefully. I woke to the smell of bacon and gentle laughter coming from the dining area. What a nice and relaxing way to wake. Not wanting to be the last one to show up for breakfast, I dressed and went out to meet my hosts.

We exchanged pleasantries and made small talk. When a few of the guests left the area and the group was smaller, I looked at the owners and told them I needed to ask a question.

David, one of the owners, was busy at the stove but nodded. I took that as my green light to ask questions.

"So, I know there is a little girl ghost here and..." I started.

"She's in the *area*, not just in the house," interjected Debby, the other owner of the house. I saw the eyes of the couple across from me grow rather large. *Not something they were expecting to discuss over breakfast*, I assumed.

Trying to be calm and matter-of-fact, I continued, "Oh, ok. Well, I was really hoping to visit with her. I even left my jewelry out, hoping she'd play with it, but no such luck."

Debby relaxed a bit, knowing that I was not going to poke the hornet's nest. "You know," started Debby, "the one I've had interactions with here is not a little girl but a young woman who was probably in her mid-twenties." *Hmmm. A young woman in her mid-twenties, I bet she would be about as tall as I am and would most likely **wear a cloak!***

"Interesting," I said. "The one I want to know about is,

well... is there a **man** here? When I was walking up the front path yesterday, I looked straight up, and I saw a man up in the window. And he was laughing at me!"

David stopped scrambling the eggs for a moment; cutting his eyes, he looked over at Debby.

"You saw a man? Upstairs?" she asked.

"Yeah! I saw him when I was walking up the path. He was in the window, he had the sheers pulled back, and he was snickering at me. He was covering his mouth and just laughing. I could see his shoulders shaking. I told him, *Don't be rude; come down and help me.* I blinked and looked again, and he was gone. Then I was walking around to the door, and I saw him again! He was STILL laughing at me. I mean, what the heck? This time, I saw him long enough, I got a good look at him. I can even sketch him out."

I looked over at David, still scrambling, but now he was smiling. He looked at me and said that they often have tours through their home, and "so-called psychics" stay with them all the time. "But you know," David started, "*you are among the very few who have actually **seen** him.* In all the years, only about four people have seen him. They **hear** him all the time, but they never **see** him. He died in the house from tuberculosis."

"So what's the deal? Why was he laughing at me?" I asked.

"He wasn't laughing at you. He was *coughing*," said David.

"Oh, geez. I get it now. The sweaty, red face. The covering of his mouth and the heaving shoulders," I said.

"Oh, geez, well… now I feel bad. The poor guy was dying, and I just wanted him to come down and help me with my luggage."

Knowing that it was going to be a rainy day and there was an extremely good chance for tornadic activity, I finished my breakfast and offered to clear the tables. *Always be polite.* Debby was kind and said she would do it, but I did take this opportunity to stay around a few more minutes and chat with her, exchanging a few "ghost war stories". It is always refreshing to meet people who have had similar positive experiences such as I have had. I am happy to see that the "fright" of the paranormal is lessening and is slowly becoming more "just a part of life".

After the fantastic breakfast, I quickly gathered my gear and began to load my car. I still needed to set up my vendor area and wanted to have everything completed before the weather shifted. As I was putting the last of my bags into my car, Debby came out to say goodbye.

"You know," she started. "I totally had forgotten about this. David actually remembered it and reminded me just now. But when we first bought the house, we had business cards made. A friend of ours came out and took photos of the house, and this is the one we went with. For the longest, people would look at the card and say they saw a man standing in the upstairs window."

"What?" I said. "Really!?"

"Yeah," said Debby. "We always laughed it off and said that it was just the reflection of the big maple tree in the yard, but we cut that tree down years ago. It's not there now, so what you saw couldn't have been a reflection."

I went over to look at the card she was holding. In the top window, the very same window, it appears to be a little short man leaning on the side of the window frame and looking through the sheers. I tried to remain calm, but I think I must have eeked out a sound of delight. Internally, I was dancing around and giving myself a one-hand psychic high five. "That's exactly where I saw him, too," I said to Debby. "Leaning on the side of the window." I could not help but beam with excitement, my cheeks turning as red as the cheeks of the little man in the too-big suit.

CHAPTER 18

HAYWOOD HOUSE

*T*ucked away on the back side of Jefferson, down by the river, stands a two-story red-brick building called the Haywood House. It is easily identified by the iconic "Golden Era" mural that is painted on the side. Like many things in Jefferson, the mural has two meanings. To some, it represents the "Golden Era" of Jefferson, when steamboats flowed down the bayou and life was filled with riches. To others it's a bit more "matter of fact" and is a tribute to one of the more opulent steamboats, aptly named the *Golden Era*, that traveled the waters.

Built as a hotel by a Confederate general in 1865, this building has stood silently in the shadows of the great trees that line the bank. Originally a four-story brick and wrought-iron building, the Haywood House was deliberately set on fire in 1872, destroying the top two floors. Since that time the Haywood House has been a private residence, a museum and is now a restaurant and cocktail bar. During the most recent renovations, several original structures were uncovered. Beneath the building is a tunnel that runs down to the river. One can imagine what was passed through the tunnel under the cloak of darkness. In another area, the original cistern was discovered and has been incorporated into the dining experience. Called the *Cistern Well Room & the Snug Booth*, stories of the past seem to merge through the opening and into this reality.

Like so many homes and buildings from the Civil War period, tragedy was not a stranger to the Haywood House. There are many reports of individuals, unable to find the answers they were seeking, jumping to their death from the fourth-floor balconies. There is even an account of a Union soldier walking out a second-floor window one night and "mysteriously dying". Ponder that for a moment. A Union soldier walks out the second-floor window in a hotel owned by a Confederate general. Interesting.

While I was visiting Jefferson, a friend of mine excitedly ran up and told me we had the "well room for the night". On my previous trip to Jefferson, I had not been able to visit the Haywood House, and I was not familiar with the history. Cocking my head like a puppy, I looked at her and, in a trademarked Mr. Spock fashion, raised one eyebrow.

"You don't *KNOW* about the well room?" she asked, astounded that I was clueless.

"No, sorry, I really don't," I replied. "I wasn't able to make it there when I came earlier in the year."

"You're going to love it! Anyone who is as psychic and sensitive and in touch with Spirit as you are—"

I waved her off, mid-sentence. I did not want to know any more. "I like to go in cold. I'd rather not know anything beforehand. I'm learning how to trust the voices, how to figure it out, and decipher what they are telling me. It's a validation thing for me."

She nodded and understood.

It's the way I have always been. Going in with information about an event, a supposed haunting, always felt deceptive. I have always tried to go in and make my own observations, seeing how accurate I am. If she was this excited about "the well", then I knew it must be good. I was instructed to meet everyone at the Haywood House for dinner. Saying a brief goodbye, I returned to my hotel to freshen up.

A storm was on its way, an extremely dangerous storm filled with lightning, high winds, hail, and tornadoes. It was adding to the atmosphere of the town. *Where's Vincent Price? He must be here somewhere?* Alerts and warnings were going off on my phone constantly, so I decided to arrive a few minutes early. If this brick building had been standing since the Civil War, I felt it was a well built and secure building, the perfect place to take shelter if a tornado decided to join us for dinner.

Once inside, I was led through the dining room and into a smaller, sectioned-off area at the top of four steps.

To my astonishment, in the center of the room was a brick well with a large and thick piece of glass over the top opening. Eight chairs circled the well, eight place settings and candles throughout the tiny room. *This must be why they call it the "snug room". By the end of the night, we were all going to be good friends.*

Shortly after I was seated, the rest of the group arrived.

Lit from deep down inside, by leaning forward one could look down into the well. Thanks in part to the storm, which was now raging outside, a strange condensation began building up on the inside of the glass tabletop. Large droplets of water clung to the glass, creating images akin to a Rorschach ink blot. Taking turns, we each placed our phones in the center of the table and challenged each other to see who could get the most unique photo.

My friend began to tell the stories of the Haywood House, and before she could really begin, the voices told me the answer to the secret of the well. Feeling a wave of "knowing" wash over the top of my head, I gasped and covered my mouth. I just looked at her; she looked at me. "What?" she asked.

"I know. I know what happened," I said. Again she asked, "What?"

I looked at her and told her, "There's a baby down there, a little baby girl. And another girl." She asked me how I knew. "They told me. The voices told me." She seemed confused and asked, "What voices? When?"

"Just now. They just told me. There's a little baby girl

down there, and there's also another little girl there. She fell in and drowned."

My friend looked at me and smiled, telling me I was correct. According to the local legend, there was a young unwed girl who had a baby. It is unclear as to who did it, but the baby was dropped into the well shortly after being born.

I was also able to see another girl, years later, accidentally falling into the well and drowning. There were no stories about this poor soul, but I would wager if all the other information given to me by the voices was accurate, then this must be as *well*.

CHAPTER 19

SATURDAY NIGHT FERVOR

illed with a packed schedule of speakers and vendors on Saturday, the town opens up several venues for group investigations on Saturday night. This is a chance to enter buildings in the historic district, some of which date back to the Civil War and Reconstruction Period, and even a few private residences.

In what could almost be equated to a paranormal speed-dating event, we were allotted a small amount of time in each venue. A five-minute window of travel time was built into the tight schedule, but unless you are extremely familiar with the town, the distances are too great to walk in five minutes. No taxi service, no Uber, and a town so dark, hiding streets that bend in an unnatural fashion, one could easily be lost if they did not know where they were heading. Streetlights are all but nonexistent in Jefferson, and it becomes an impossibility to read the dim and faded street signs. We were left with no other viable alternative than to supply our own method of transportation. We stepped up to the challenge—and rented golf carts.

Our first venue of the night was the Claiborne House, a bed and breakfast in Jefferson. Quietly we gathered on the steps of the front of the house. Residual Halloween decorations haunted the home, but one could tell, on Monday the winter holiday decorations would be up. While standing on the steps, I met a very nice woman and her nephew. The three of us struck up a conversation, and I found that her nephew was a budding intuitive. Realizing this was an opportunity to jump in and hopefully steer him away from the "reality" of paranormal entertainment television, I started speaking with him, asking questions—one intuitive to another. I found out a few of our methods were the same, but as Teal L. Gray said, *"The only difference is verbiage."*

I could feel a woman, an elderly spirit, dressed in gray, standing not too far from me, behind me and to my left. She was clear, and I could see her with my third eye. "Do you feel anything out here?" I asked the nephew. He thought for a moment and said yes. Turning the adventure into a game, we decided to "challenge" each other and see how many times we felt something in the same place. Asking where he felt the spiritual energy, he pointed over my left shoulder just as I began to point in the same direction. I smiled, wanting to show him that feeling the energy of residual spirits was not out of the ordinary. Back to the first law of thermodynamics we go. *Energy only changes.*

There were approximately thirty of us waiting in the damp air for the doors to open. When they opened, we were greeted by none other than Natalie Jones, CEO of ParaFLIXX. Natalie led us to the small kitchen, where we grabbed something warm to drink and then headed into the formal dining room for the investigation.

After a few moments of listening to our host explain the equipment, I realized this was not a true investigation, rather an introduction for those who had never participated in one. Excusing myself from the area, I stepped to the back of the crowd and allowed others to share in the experience. At the back of the group, I reconnected with my new friends from the steps. The young nephew was running around with a K2 meter.

Pointing up the stairs, I indicated he should go up there. "That's where they are; they're at the top of the stairs. They're not down here with all these people; they're up there. And there is also a lady who is moving around the perimeter of the house outside. She's staying near the gardens, near the flowers. I think she was the 'lady of the house', and the gardens is where she was the happiest, working with the flowers."

With his K2 meter in hand, the young nephew walked quietly up the stairs and disappeared for a few minutes. I took a seat in the front room and looked around, taking in the sights of the house. Within a few minutes the young nephew was walking back down the stairs, almost exploding with excitement. He began to tell me how the meter started lighting up and reacting when he got to the top of the stairs. He was able to document energy spikes where there were none before. Knowing that he will be walking down the right path, and not the over sensationalized one, I nodded and smiled. I do feel that he was rather surprised at the matter-of-fact approach I was taking, staying calm the entire time. This approach will serve him well in the future, allowing for logical experiments into the world of the unseen.

After thirty minutes, our group was ushered out the door and on to the next "investigation". Stepping outside, I saw a friend of mine had his golf cart nearby. Offering to give me a ride, I decided to experience the "full Jefferson", hopped on the back of the cart, and sped into the mist, headed to our next destination.

Before I realized it, we were pacing another cart, and suddenly we found ourselves in a heated golf cart drag race down the main strip of the closed-up town. The roads, still wet from the storm before, became a derailed roller-coaster ride. Every bump and dip in the road became an instant log flume. Obviously the inspiration for *The Fast and the Furious 3*, we discovered in the moonless night that drifting became easier, aided by the four of us leaning to one side of the golf cart. *"The joyfulness of the paranormal."*

The second "investigation" was the same, a demonstration into dowsing rods. We sat around a living room and watched someone else speak and then demonstrate the rods. My friends and I began to exchange side glances, indicating that we were all thinking the same thing. For those of us who have spent countless hours in the dark, only to follow it with even more endless hours reviewing audio and video clips, these were not real investigations, at least not to us. They were a magnificent introduction for those who have never experienced this in the past. When we were released, we hopped back on to our midnight chariot, mapless, and again drove through the darkness of Jefferson, looking for our next destination.

When we arrived at the third venue, we were greeted by a centurion guarding the door to the warehouse. The group that arrived before us was a rather large group, much larger than ours, and they were running about forty-five minutes behind schedule. We sat on the benches lining the buildings and decided we would wait for a bit, but only a bit. The centurion, trying his best to entertain the growing crowd, gave a brief introduction to their paranormal group. *"We've been investigating together for two years,"* he went on to say. Exhaustion of the day was setting in, and I could not help but roll my eyes and start to walk away.

"Victoria! Where are you *going?*" asked a friend.

Shaking my head, I looked at her and said, "Two years? Two *YEARS?* My **shoes** are older than that." We all began

to laugh and realized that our small group had more experience than the majority of those leading the "investigations". Deciding that they should be able to have their own
fun, we piled back into the golf cart and headed back to
the Jefferson, knowing where to go for real adventures.

CHAPTER 20

WHY IS JEFFERSON SO HAUNTED?

*J*efferson, Texas, was a Wild West riverfront town. Steamboats, shuttling between New Orleans and Jefferson, began regular routes in the early 1840s. Along with the wealth and fortunes that landed on the shores of the Big Cypress Bayou, another element was introduced to the growing town. The darker side of life—gambling, prostitution, murder, slavery, and crime—took root on the banks of the river and slowly began creeping into the town. Many of the buildings that remain in the historic district were all necessities of the time. Cotton warehouses, banks, brothels, drugstores, and saloons lined the streets, witnessing the corruptions of life.

After the Civil War, there were several fires that raged through Jefferson. One fire in particular, "the 1869 Fire", burned and destroyed approximately thirty buildings in the historic downtown area. So much loss and destruction for a small section of the town. Locals began calling it the "Million-Dollar Fire".

As with so many legendary places upon this earth that we call "haunted", it is the blood and emotions that stain the land, creating a ripple in the ether. Much like a piece of mica, layers upon layers of realities, dimensions and realms lie on top of each other, thin sheet upon thin sheet. To look at a layer individually, it appears thin and fragile, almost veil-like in appearance. When combined with other layers, individual beams of light are not able to penetrate the stone. Only the layer directly in front of a person can be seen—unless, of course, one shifts their perspective and begins to look at life and the world with new eyes. By taking the piece of mica, shifting it a degree and holding it to the light, one can begin to see how individual layers combine with each other and make a complete stone. The vibrational frequency of the stone is altered by the addition of the light source, and individual layers become translucent and easier to see. Exactly like the piece of mica, our lives are made of not one individual layer, but many layers combined. There are some, such as myself, who see the individuality of the layers comprising the reality of the stone. Others only see when the stone is held to a light source, the veil thinned, if you will. The layers are always there, always present, but many cannot or choose not to see. Close a blind eye if you must, but the reality still remains.

Within this area of Texas, there is still a strong Confederate feel. Like so many towns in this corner of the state, Jefferson is no exception. Antebellum mansions with graceful gardens can still be found throughout the town, reminding passersby of the beauty and grace that was once alive. There is an impenetrable pre-Civil War Southern feel in the town. It goes unspoken, but the reality still remains. A statue of a Confederate soldier stands vigilantly on duty on the corner of Polk and Austin Streets, forever on alert and guarding the Marion County Courthouse. Faded photos of Confederate generals and soldiers adorn the walls of restaurants and bars dotted throughout the town; a larger-than-life Robert E. Lee portrait adorns the walls of Auntie Skinner's Riverboat Club, a local restaurant and bar. Dim reminders of a way of life that walked the streets of Jefferson not that long ago. Streets, cemeteries and family names of the Confederacy live on in this little town deep in Northeast Texas.

There is a weighted darkness that can be felt hanging over the streets, palpable to even those who are not sensitive to the energies that exist beyond the veil. Like pools of water seeking the lowest point to gather, shadow figures seek refuge, haunting the corners of darkness. There is no mistaking the feeling one gets at night. Jefferson was a pre-Civil War town and was vehemently pro-slavery during the Civil War.

As I walked the town lit mainly by the growing moon, it was impossible to tell the actual year. I wandered the streets alone that night, stopping when shadows moved. I somehow expected to see a man in a gray suit step from the corner of the dimly lit night. Silhouettes, darker than dark, seemed to be centered in the contoured edges of the property lines. It became increasingly more difficult to tell what was a shadow created by the bright moon and what could possibly be *a shadow* created by another realm.

Today, the modern townspeople are kind and friendly, welcoming visitors into their quaint and charming town. To the citizens of Jefferson, history lives only in the past and seldom gives it a second thought. If one were to stand on a high vantage point and watch the town below, they would see the local citizens disappear one by one before sunset, locking the past and the darkness outside of their homes. Houses glowing from inside, many antebellum in nature, timeless on a dark and cloudless night. As the moon rises, there is a different feel about the town. History rises, takes form, and begins to walk down the vacant streets and into the buildings that existed when Jefferson was a new and bustling town. The night breathes a sigh once again, and with it, there is a para-normal changing of the guards. The veil is lifted, and the world is forever reborn.

Why is Jefferson so haunted? The town, this entire area of the state, silently echoes the pains that were felt during the Civil War. The Confederacy, slavery, riverboats and railroads, all parts of our past that are now glossed over in textbooks, lived in the earliest days of this town. Emotions and blood that are locked into the land still echo; vibrations so subtle, resonating as undertones, can still be felt as one walks down the streets and into the buildings. This area of Texas, almost equal in the pain, heartache and emotions that were felt on battlefields, goes unmarked. Everyone I spoke with agrees, this is why Jefferson is so haunted, haunted because of the scars and blood on the land. History is not in the past—history is alive and just waiting for a chance to be seen and heard by those who are able to listen.

ABOUT THE AUTHOR

Author and Paranormal Radio Host Victoria Mundae has been described as *"spooky 'Elle Woods' rolled up in a ball of Sunshine with a dash of a Paranormal Princess thrown in for fun"*. Nicknamed the *"Paranormal Perfect Storm"*, Victoria is a contributing author to several literary compendiums and her writings have appeared in the paranormal literary journal *"The Feminine Macabre: A Woman's Journal of All Things Strange and Unusual"*. She has also been profiled in the book *"A Walk in the Shadows"* and in the TV Mini-Series, *"The Shadow Dimension"*.

In addition to writing, paranormal investigations, and embracing the "woo-woo" of life, Victoria co-hosted the long-running paranormal podcast *"Edge Of The Rabbit Hole"* and later joined the paranormal panel podcast *"Black Lotus Live"*. With hopes of helping paranormal and esoteric subjects merge into the mainstream narrative, she created the wildly popular *"Victoria Mundae's Paranormal Activity"* Activity Book Series for both adults and children.

Upon deciding to take her writing career to a higher level, Victoria has teamed up and joined forces with *"Beyond The Fray Publishing"* – a publishing house that caters specifically to the paranormal and true crime genres – and is excited to be writing in both the fiction and non-fiction paranormal genres.

facebook.com/VMundae
twitter.com/VMundae
instagram.com/Victoria_Mundae